AF540573

INQUIRY TRAINING MODEL

INQUIRY TRAINING MODEL

Author
Dr. M. VANAJA
M.Sc. (Edu.), Ph. D.
Asst. Professor
Institution of Advanced Study in Education
S. V. University, Tirupati-517 502 (A.P.)

Editor
Dr. DIGUMARTI BHASKARA RAO
M. Sc., M. A., M.A., M.Ed., Ph. D.
R. V.R. College of Education
Guntur-522 006 (A.P.)

DISCOVERY PUBLISHING HOUSE
New Delhi-110 002

First Published-1999
Reprinted: 2013

ISBN 81-7141-515-6

Published by:
DISCOVERY PUBLISHING HOUSE
4831/24, Ansari Road, Prahlad Street,
Darya Ganj, New Delhi-110 002 (*INDIA*)
Phone: 3279245
Fax: 91-11-3253475

Printed at: Dynamic printers, Delhi

This book is dedicated to my Grand Father but for whose constant motivation this would not have become a reality. I thank my parents and my husband for their constant support and encouragement throughout this academic endeavour.

Vanaja

Foreword

The present day teacher education programme has become outdated, obsolete, and ineffective. There is a great need to revitalize the programme and give it a thorough dressing by purging the dead wood and by inducing new and challenging course to meet the challenges of the present rapid growing technological society. This transformation is more needed in science teacher education programme than in any other aspect of teacher education.

While we all have the long standing knowledge of science teaching methods and techniques, no novel ideas or innovative experimentation has taken place to make these methods and techniques more and more relevant, dynamic, and effective in realizing the objectives of teaching science. The models of teaching have revolutionized the whole teaching process demanding an entirely new outlook and new orientation to teaching. These models apply very aptly and very effectively to the teaching of science, hence the need for strengthening the teacher education programme with the introduction and functioning of the model's approach.

There has been a record of several attempts by teacher educators and field researchers in verifying and highlighting the various aspects of the models of teaching in their own humble way. The present study is one such sincere and scientific piece of work on the introduction of training through model in science teacher education programme. The researcher Dr. Ms. Vanaja has made an extensive study of the models of teaching in its various forms and contexts. She has developed a systematic experimental model and made innovative and insightful advances into the field spending a great deal of her time, efforts, and scholarship.

The results are extremely thought provoking and inspirational for both In-service and Pre-service science teachers. They have far reaching implications for improving the dull and drab act of teaching of science into one of the rare dynamism, active participation involving higher levels of intellectual skills of reasoning, induction and analysis, which is the need of this hour of tremendous scientific and cybernetic growth of the modern world.

I commend her work immensely and encourage the readers to reap significant benefits from this pioneering publication of doctoral research.

Dr. T. J. Rajendra Prasad
Former Dean
Faculty of Education
Nagarjuna University
Guntur

Preface

Teacher education is a continuous process. New advances that come up on the educational horizon have to be addressed to and their implementation has to be researched upon. Innovations in teacher education programme have to correspond to needs of school system and vice versa.

This study is one such endeavour in this direction, to identify a training strategy to train student teachers in the use of Inquiry Training Model. It also attempts to find out the readiness of teacher educators to use Models of Teaching.

The body of the study is divided into five chapters. Chapter 1 deals with Teacher Education and Models of Teaching. Chapter 2 deals with Science Education and Inquiry Training Models. Chapter 3 pertains to the Review of Literature and various studies conducted by different authors and researchers. Chapter 4 deals with the Research Procedure highlighting the Objectives, Sampling Techniques, Research Design, Tools used and Data Analysis Techniques. Chapter 5 outlines the Data Analysis and Interpretation, Results and Findings, and the Conclusions. Executive Summary is given at the end for quick reference.

I am profusely indebted to Dr. T. J. Rajendra Prasad, Retd. Principal and Hony. Professor, Centre for Research in Education, A.L. College of Education, Nagarjuna University. But for his unstinted, able and encouraging guidance, and active support, the present work would not have seen the light of the day.

I am grateful to Dr. M. Syama Sundara Rao, Principal, A.L.College of Education; Dean of Education, Nagarjuna University and Mr. G. Sundara Rao, Senior Lecturer, A.L. College of Education, for their constant guidance, interaction, and encouragement.

I thank Dr. D. Bhaskara Rao, for editing the book. I am also thankful to Discovery Publishing House.

Last but not the least, I thank the teacher educators and student teachers who co-operated with me in giving the required information during data collection without which the study would not have become a reality.

Vanaja, M.

Overview

The teaching profession will have the largest number of members as compared to any other profession in any country and the teachers are the main instruments in implementing the policies formulated to achieve a breakthrough in the quantitative expansion and qualitative improvement of education.

Science education has become an integral part of human life and every one is supposed to have a minimum knowledge of scientific literacy. As science is made a compulsory subject at school level which decides the selection of many professional courses in future, it has become a dire need to science teachers to present it effectively in the class rooms.

Inquiry Training Model (ITM), developed by Robert Suchman, is one of the most effective teaching strategies of science education. It teaches the students how to learn an inquiry process and how to derive a solution to a problem. With the knowledge of ITM, a student can very easily and effectively encounter a problem and get a solution.

Recognising the role of ITM in science education, a study was undertaken to identify the knowledge of ITM and attitudes towards the use of ITM possessed by the teacher educators and student teachers as they are the people who have the opportunity of using ITM at theory and practice levels.

The teacher educators and the student teachers are willing to implement ITM in science teaching. The modular approach has been proved to be an effective strategy to train student teachers in the use of ITM. As the teacher educators and student teachers are willing to use the ITM in their teaching, it can be introduced in teacher education and science education curricula along with other models and methods of teaching.

I hope that this publication on ITM will help many a researcher, curriculum planner, teacher and student of science education.

Dr. Digumarti Bhaskara Rao

Secretary, ACCESS
D-43, S.V.N. Colony
Guntur-522 006
Andhra Pradesh (India).

CONTENTS

Foreword vii
Preface ix
Overview xi

1. TEACHER EDUCATION - MODELS OF TEACHING 1
   Introduction
   Growth and Development of teacher education in India
   Concept of teacher education
   Goals of teacher education
   Objectives of teacher education
   Present Status of teacher education in India and needed action
   Innovations in teacher education
   Models of teaching
   Conclusion

2. SCIENCE EDUCATION – INQUIRY TRAINING MODEL 30
   Introduction
   Goals of Science Education
   Approaches To Science Teaching
   Inquiry Teaching / Types of Inquiry
   Suchman's Inquiry Training Model
   Rationale of the Study
   Research Questions of the Study
   Objectives of the Study
   Working assumptions of the Study
   Limitations of the Study
   Title of the Study

3. REVIEW OF RELATED LITERATURE 52
   Introduction
   Studies Related to Inquiry Teaching in Schools
   Studies Related to Pre Service Teacher Education

In Models of Teaching
Studies Related to Teacher Educators Attitudes Towards Innovations / Models of Teaching
Conclusion

4. RESEARCH PROCEDURE 85
Introduction
Research Design
Sampling Procedures Used
Experiment Design
Experimental Validity
Selection of Experimenter
Tools Used in the Study
Data Analysis Techniques
Conclusion

5. DATA ANALYSIS AND INTERPRETATION 100
Introduction
Teacher Educators Response to Willingness Scale
Student Teachers Response Data to: Theory Check Up, Reaction Scale, and Willingness Scale
Discussion
Conclusion

6. SUMMARY SUGGESTIONS FOR FURTHER STUDY AND RECOMMENDATIONS 130

BIBLIOGRAPHY 141

APPENDIX 155

Teacher Education and Models of Teaching

INTRODUCTION

The professional education of teachers is an essential component for the qualitative improvement of education. This has been stressed time and again by different education commissions.

According to Education Commission (1964-66), "A sound programme of professional education of teachers is essential for the qualitative improvement of education. Investment in teacher education can yield very rich dividends because the financial resources required are small when measured against the resulting improvement in the education of millions."

Even the UNESCO-ILO document (1967) on the status of teachers emphatically states that "It should be recognized that advance in education depends largely on the qualification and ability of the teaching staff in general and on the human, pedagogical and technical qualities of the individual teachers."

J.C. Aggarwal (1995) has aptly asserted the relevance of teacher education for the betterment of society as "If we educate a boy we educate one individual, if we educate a girl, we educate the whole family, and if we educate a teacher, we educate the whole community."

The role of a teacher in a modern industrial society is entirely different from the traditional agrarian society. He has to prepare students for the type of society in which he has to lead his future life. Not only does he have to take note of the demands of the society, but also has to take responsibility of developing proper values, attitudes and skills in children.

Only tactful, resourceful, highly educated and equipped persons can effectively cope with the changing situations.

B.R. Purkait (1987) stressing on the importance of teacher education opines that "If a nation wants quality education, it must have quality teachers. The quality of a nation depends on the quality of its schools. The quality of schools depends primarily on the quality of teachers."

J.B. Conant (1963) states that "The united effort of all teacher educators would help to prepare better teachers, which would result in better schools requires no augmentation; that the nation would be the beneficiary of such a revolution is self-evident proposition."

DEVELOPMENT OF TEACHER EDUCATION IN INDIA

'Teaching to be taught and trained' – is a relatively new growing concept found in societies all over the world, in nineteenth and twentieth centuries. Prior to this period, teaching existed as an art in all countries and communities.

Much before any need for a special group of people was felt, they existed in varied forms suitable for varied occupations. While the parents and elders taught the youngsters the art of living, the tribal headsman, the craftsman, and skilled worker imparted to them specialised skills. The technique of the teacher that was often based on his acquired expertise over the years got transmitted to the learner. The student would be declared qualified not by any institution or organization but by the teacher alone. The testimony of the worth of such transmission lay entirely on the pupil's use of skill learnt. The teacher's recognition automatically came from the learners' performance.

In religious teaching the role of a teacher was that of a spiritual master. The teacher utilized his vast repertoire of experience and skills to impart knowledge to his students. The communication was usually one way and the students' reaction was almost absent.

Ancient Past

In ancient past, the teacher's role was directed towards the worldly and spiritual welfare of the learner. The Guru was held in high esteem and the task (teaching) was widely revered. The teacher was expected to be the master of a specific branch or branches of studies and also have a high moral character.

The Rig-Veda prescribes that for the preparation of 'Gurus', it was necessary that he should possess:

(i) A scholarly bent of mind;
(ii) High degree of intelligence;
(iii) Devotion to acquire mastery of the subject;
(iv) Ability to live through an austere life;
(v) The will to live the life of a Brahmacharin; and
(vi) An ardent belief in the supreme God and supreme goodness.

It was believed that a 'Guru' had to realize within himself the truth of every aspect of knowledge by self-introspection. It was only then that he would be in a position to lead the learner through the path of realization. The test of his ability was seen in skill of teaching, explaining, exposure, illustration, interpreting, and expounding knowledge in relation to his experiences. Disciples flocked around the efficient preceptor. There was no formal teacher-training course or recognized institution.

Medieval Period

Education was imparted in pathashalas and in madarasas. Education was essentially of a religious nature with emphasis on the study of classical languages, grammar, and scriptures and in lower classes the study of the 3 Rs. For teaching in these institutions a formal training of teachers was non-existent. It was commonly believed that if a person knew his subject well, he could as well teach it.

The 'monitorial' system was in vogue in the fourteenth and fifteenth century. The expert eye of the 'Guru' used to detect the few talented scholars who were senior in intellect and bent on the pursuit of knowledge. This small group got some impetus from their teachers who would detain them in the school for a longer period and make them competent to take over charge of the younger and mediocre students. The batch of monitors, the intermediaries gained gradually in maturity and knowledge, acquired ability in taking charge of the younger colleagues and this brought in the element of teacher education. For the first time in the history of teacher education, the true teacher was conceived to be as one who was well versed in scriptures and theology, skilful in the art of exposition, and one who had acquired a well integrated personality and who used to command respect.

Early British Period

The spread of teacher education in the country down the centuries can be traced to the references made to it by Historians and Members of Public Instruction of East India Company. With all the weakness that had crept into the then prevalent system, some obvious merits were appreciated by them.

G.L. Prendergast (1827) observed that "I need hardly mention what every member of the Board knows as well as I do, that there is hardly a village, great or small, throughout our territories in which there is not at least one school and in larger villages more; many in every division where young natives are taught writing, reading and arithmetic upon a system so economical, from a handful or two of grain to perhaps a rupee per month to the school master, according to the ability of the parents and at the same time so simple and effectual, that there is hardly a cultivator or petty dealer who is not competent to keep his own accounts with a degree of accuracy in my opinion beyond what we meet with amongst the lower orders in our country; whilst the more splendid dealers and bankers keep their books with a degree of ease, consciousness and clearness I rather think fully equal to those of any British merchant.

Many British officers supported this view of having some merit in the indigenous system of education.

A.D. Campbell's (then Collector of Bellary, Province of Madras) report incorporates quite a detailed account of the spread and qualitative standard of education in that district. There were 533 schools (primary) containing no more than 6, 641 scholars.... Besides these there were 23 places of instruction attended by Brahmins exclusively in which some of the Hindu sciences such as theology, astronomy, logic, and law were taught in Sanskrit language. In these places of Sanskrit instruction, attended by youth and often by persons far advanced in life, education, was conducted on a plan entirely different from that pursued in schools in which children were taught reading, writing, and arithmetic only in several vernacular dialects of the country. Elaborating on the method of Instruction, he adds that when the whole scholars were assembled, the scholars according to their numbers and attainments were divided into several classes, the lower ones were partly under the care of the monitors, while the higher ones were more directly under the superintendence of the master.

But there is no evidence to show that any form of teacher education existed till the first decade of nineteenth century, excepting for the monitorial system.

Early Nineteenth Century

Late in the eighteenth century, foreign missionaries had started a few training institutes essentially for the primary grade teachers. The first school mentioned was a normal school established by Dr. Kare in Serampore (Bengal). The teachers were trained for primary stage and got trained in vernacular medium. The monitorial system was recommended for adoption and came to be called the Bell-Lancaster system.

In 1828, the Women Committee of Calcutta opened a training centre for ladies. In 1825, Sir Thomas Monroe, the Governor of Madras Presidency opened a Central School in Madras. He reported that 'without a body of better instructed teachers than we have at present, no progress can be made'. A number of training schools were opened in Lahore, Madras, Bombay, etc., in the period 1859 to 1882. The chief aims of teacher training institutions were:

(i) A selected group of youth would acquire specialization in teacher training.
(ii) The training consisted mainly of content enrichment with very little teaching practice or experience.

(iii) Trainees would be awarded certificates on completion of training and
arrangements would be made for their employment.

The Hunter Commission also known as Indian Education Commission (1882) was directed to inquire into the quality and character of instructions imparted in schools for secondary education. Suggestions were made regarding teacher education:

1. Institution of a system of examination into the principles and practice required for qualifying in the teacher-training course.
2. The selection of candidates (graduates and undergraduates) for courses of study.
3. Duration of two types of courses for two different groups.
4. Condition of employment in a school.

By 1902, the need for professional preparation for school-teachers was fairly recognized. The Education Act of 1902 in England initiated the qualitative improvement of education through training programmes of teachers.

The educational policy in 1904 under Lord Curzon emphasized the need for expansion of training programmes. The resolution of 1904 declared that 'if the teaching in secondary schools is to be raised to a higher level, if the pupils are to be cured of their tendency to rely on learning notes and text books by heart. If, in a word, European knowledge is to be diffused by the methods proper to it, then it is necessary that the teachers themselves should be trained in the art of teaching.'

The resolution drew the attention of provincial governments to recruit trained teachers in schools and to have better staff in the training colleges which were to be equipped with libraries and museums. The training colleges were to have practice teaching schools attached to them and under their control. The courses were to be chiefly directed towards imparting to the student teachers the knowledge of principles that underlie the art of teaching and some degree of technical skills in the practice of the art. The practical training was to embrace the extension, consolidation, and revision of general studies to make the student teachers capable teachers. This resolution gave a fillip to growth of teacher education colleges in different parts of the country.

The policy of expansion was further strengthened by the declaration of 1913. The declaration was 'Eventually under modern system of education no teacher should be allowed to teach without a certificate that he is qualified to do so'.

It laid emphasis on free interchange of ideas on the success or failures of experiments and determination of the methods to be used in practical work. It also underscored the relative importance of methodology and of study of psychology.

The Calcutta University Commission (1917) under the chairmanship of Sir Michael Saddler made certain important recommendations regarding teacher education. It recommended the establishment of university education departments for training of teachers. It suggested that in addition to the practice teaching school, there should be small experimental school attached to every training college. The school could be used for trying out experiments in the methods and techniques of teaching to make education a university subject (Research oriented).

Thus, the period between 1904-40 highlighted the following features:

(i) The teacher training got reoriented on more progressive lines.
(ii) The number of training colleges and student enrolment showed a remarkable increase.
(iii) Refresher courses such as in-service programmes for teacher were started.
(iv) Researchers in education were encouraged.
(v) Provision of infra-structural facilities—viz., libraries, laboratories, practicing schools and qualified staff, etc., was stressed upon .

The Central Advisory Board of Education (C.A.B.E.) surveyed the main fields of educational activities during the post war period in India. The report submitted under the chairmanship of Sir John Sargent categorically stated "It is for India to decide whether the time has arrived when a national system of education is a paramount necessity."

Post Independence Period

The University Education Commission set up in 1948, under the chairmanship of Dr. Radhakrishnan to review (apart from other questions of higher education) secondary education in particular. The Commission noted that the theoretical courses were stereotyped. In some cases the contents were stereotyped and in some cases the contents were even vague and unrelated to the actual classroom conditions. It suggested that the theory courses in education should be flexible and adaptable to local circumstances. It recommended 12 weeks of practice teaching with more emphasis on training in school practices in vogue.

The Secondary Education Commission (1952-53) stressed upon the importance of teaching practice. The Commission recommended the setting up of multipurpose schools with diversified courses for which teachers were to be given specialised training. The Commission reiterated the utility of having a demonstration school/model school attached to each training institution. They were fully aware of the fact that the development of practical ability in a teacher should depend upon two basic things:

(i) Teaching comprising lesson planning, preparation, delivery, and encouragement to the students for participation. In short a command of knowledge of the subject and skill in handling it besides observation, demonstration, and criticism of lessons.
(ii) Sessional practice work including activities that strengthen and enrich teaching such as construction and administration of scholastic tests, organization of supervised study and student societies, conducting library periods and maintenance of cumulative records.

In 1955, All India Council for Secondary Education was established to suggest improvement and expansion of secondary education. The Council through its departments of extension services planned to improve school practices by active participation of teachers in service.

The beginning of sixties saw several big changes in the field of teacher education—the formation of NCERT, the establishment of four Regional Colleges of Education, the starting of B.Ed. Correspondence course to clear backlog of secondary school teachers and part-time M.Ed. courses in several universities. Education Commission (1964-66) was set up to go into the whole system of education—university, secondary, primary, and teacher education. The Commission realized the importance of professional education preparation of teachers for qualitative improvement of education. The Commission recommended the revision of courses in light of the fundamental objectives of preparing teachers for their varied responsibilities in an evolving system of education.

The National Workshop at Shimla in May 1976 and Regional Workshop at Madras in November 1976 discussed teacher education programmes at different levels. The deliberations of the above were discussed in a National Conference of Teacher Education held in New Delhi in February, 1977, organized by NCERT and UGC. The recommendations were published in a monograph called "Teacher Education Curriculum—A Framework". They have suggested reorganization of teacher education programmes in three broad areas: (i) Pedagogical theory; (ii) Community work, and (iii) Content-cum-methodology (including practice teaching and practical work).

The Committees had made the following observations regarding the teacher training programmes 'whatever the reasons, the teacher training institutions stand isolated from the mainstream of national life, from the academic life of the university, from schools, from one another and what is more from the very community, at once requires the greatest significance in view of the changed political and socio-economic situation in the country. It tried to project a new look to student teaching in which new practices like micro teaching and simulation in teaching were advocated to be included in teacher education programmes.'

The National Commission on Secondary Teaching (1983-85) under the chairmanship of Prof. D.P. Chattopadhyaya has made wide-ranging recommendations on teacher education programmes.

It advocated either four or five years integrated programme after senior secondary leading to graduation and training. The course content would consist of 2 elements (i) General education and (ii) Professional preparation.

General education was to include:

(i) Study of languages
(ii) Three or four disciplines from amongst school subjects
(iii) Seminars, projects and study visits.

Professional education was to include:

(i) Study of education as a discipline including educational psychology, sociology and philosophy of education.
(ii) Practice of teaching and its content-cum-methodology.
(iii) Learning of a variety of skills related to the role of the teacher including educational technology and preparation of software.
(iv) Duration of internship to be of four weeks in third year and three weeks in fourth year. During this period stress would be laid among other things on blackboard writing, drawing skills, making and improvising aids, and to learning and using technological equipment.
(v) Participation in co-curricular activities like games, sports, music, dance, etc., were to be made obligatory.

The Commission recommended for a wide scale modification in the teacher education curriculum.

The National Policy on Education—1986 was modified in 1992. The main recommendations pertaining to teacher education were:

1. Teacher Education is a continuous process and its pre- service and in-service components are inseparable. As a first step, the entire teacher education has to be overhauled.
2. The new programme of teacher education was proposed to emphasize continuing education. The teachers were to be motivated to fulfil the thrusts envisaged in the policy.
3. Establishment of District Institutes of Education and Training was one of the main thrust areas. The DIETs were to organize pre service courses for elementary school teachers and for the personnel working in non-formal and adult education centres.

It was envisaged that the establishment of DIETs would eventually lead to the phasing out of the substandard institutions. It was proposed to upgrade certain selected secondary teacher education colleges to complement the functioning of SCERTs. Provision was to be made to provide the National Council of Teacher Education with necessary resources. Networking arrangements were to be created between institutions of teacher education and University departments of education.

National Council for Teacher Education (NCTE) has been in existence for more than two decades and has been made a statutory body (1995). It's important functions are:

1. To advice the Government of India on all matters concerning teacher education, including pre service and in service education, evaluation of curricula for teacher education and periodical review of progress in revising the curriculum.
2. To advice the state governments on any matters referred to the council by them.
3. To review the progress of plan schemes both central and state concerning teacher education.
4. To advise government on ensuring adequate standards in teacher education.
5. Any other matter entrusted to the council by Government of India.

CONCEPT OF THE TERM TEACHER EDUCATION

Teacher education can be briefly denoted as: "Teacher Education = Teacher + Education = Education for teachers according to R.A. Sharma (1989). Further, Sharma opines that "Teacher education covers those theoretical aspects through which knowledge pertaining to specific subjects is transmitted to students and teachers are prospected. Teacher education includes all those activities, operations and events through which the prospective teachers are to be made aware of the latest trends of teaching and subject knowledge. It should give them a thorough knowledge of the learner's behavioural changes and management techniques. The student teacher is subjected to formal and informal situations that lead to development of communication and teaching skills. Finally, the most important of all, it develops in student teachers an interest in teaching and respect for the teaching profession."

B.O. Smith (1969) opines that "If a student is to be prepared for the evolving world, then an essential attribute of effective teacher is an awareness of the realities of the world. Smith also contends that the essence of teacher education should be that of preparation for life in the society."

A.O. Toffler (1973) has outlined the role of future teachers in these words "It is no longer sufficient for Johnny to understand the past. It is not even enough for him to understand the present, for the 'here and now' environment will soon vanish. Johnny must learn to anticipate the new directions and the rate of change and so must Johnny's teachers."

The UNESCO document "Learning To Be" (1972) made the following comments on teacher education. 'Pedagogical training must be geared to knowing and respecting the multiple aspects of human personality'. It emphasizes on 'What was once an art' – the art of teaching is now a science, built on firm foundations and linked to psychology, anthropology, cybernetics, linguistics and many other disciplines. UNESCO recommends that 'conditions in which teachers are trained should be profoundly changed, so that they essentially become educators rather than specialists in transmitting pre-established curricula; the principle of a first accelerated training stage, followed by in service training cycles should be adopted.'

According to B.R. Purkait (1987) teacher education means professional preparation of a teacher. He states that "Teacher education must lead to the acquisition of the type of knowledge or information, skill and ability which helps a teacher to discharge his professional duties and responsibilities effectively and efficiently. He adds that teacher education implies reshaping the attitudes, habits, and personality of a teacher."

J.C. Aggarwal (1995) refers to all programmes/strategies/tactics as a result of which a prospective teacher is able to help his pupils to acquire learning – cognitive, psychomotor, and affective as teacher education.

R.K. Srivastava and K. Bose (1973) define teacher education as "An activity that needs a process to explain it, a goal to determine its achievement and a doer to perform it. Further they state that the teacher education should deal with the questions – (i) Who the performers or would be educator are? (ii) How does one educate them to be teachers? (iii) What skills and knowledge and behaviour patterns should they be expected to develop?

The above definitions of teacher education points that teacher education should have the following characteristic features:

(i) To enable the students to understand the process of teaching-learning activity.

(ii) To gain knowledge about latest trends and techniques of teaching.
(iii) To enrich ones subject content knowledge.
(iv) To develop teaching and communication skills
(v) To prepare student-teachers for life in society
(vi) To enable one to perceive the environment in which one lives
(vii) To develop various facets of human personality
(viii) To enable him to train to discharge his professional duties and responsibilities effectively and efficiently.
(ix) To develop respect for teaching profession.

The process of teacher education can be represented diagrammatically as in Fig. 1.1:

Fig. 1

Representation of Teacher Education

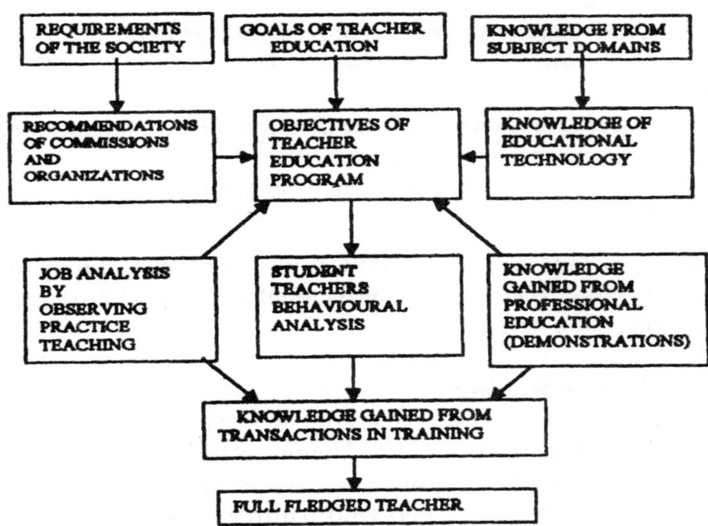

The education of teachers is an integral part of the educational system, which itself is closely linked with the social system. Any curriculum of teacher education, which is not in conformity with the changing educational and social realities, will finally become unproductive. Thus ideally speaking, the educational system has to be developed and designed to meet the requirements of its own society. Thus any change in the society has to be reflected in the educational system which in turn has to be incorporated in the teacher education curriculum.

GOALS OF TEACHER EDUCATION

The goals of teacher education as identified by NCTE are:

1. To Strengthen National Integration:

The constitutional obligation of the state is to establish a secular socialistic democratic society in which all citizens are to be guaranteed equality of status and opportunity, freedom, and justice. For achieving these objectives the courses should be forward looking, just and progressive. Some of the issues that call for immediate attention are:

(i) To strengthen national and social cohesion in a diverse and plural society,
(ii) To accelerate the process of economic growth,
(iii) To improve the life of the downtrodden and people living below the poverty line,
(iv) To remove the widely prevalent ignorance, superstition and prejudices from the masses, and
(v) To inculcate scientific temper and develop a critical awareness about the realities of Indian life.

The teachers and teacher educators have a special role to play in this venture. They need to train student teachers to be in a position to satisfy these national goals.

2. To Promote Secularism:

India is a secular country. Herein, religious education and teacher education are powerful means of promoting secular consciousness among teachers who in turn would promote the same among their pupils.

3. To Facilitate Human Resource and Economic Development:

Education is an effective means for both human resource and economic development. The attitude towards 'manual labour' has to be transformed. Dignity of labour and morality of workmanship will have to be inculcated. The vocationalization of education and the introduction of Socially Useful Productive Work (SUPW) in schools have to be given a meaningful direction

4. To Arrest the Alienation of Educated Youth from Society and Unemployment:

The flight of educated rural youth from the villages to the city makes cities overcrowded and over populated. In turn it makes the rural areas devoid of skilled, trained, and educated manpower. The fruits of education are not infiltrating into the village community. In the cities the young are marginalised. They face problems of unemployment, adjustment, acceptability, and habitation leading to alienation. Thus teacher education programmes should reorient the youth to transact the methods in any situation rural/urban.

GENERAL OBJECTIVES OF TEACHER EDUCATION

The general objectives of teacher education as listed in the Curriculum Framework for Teacher Education by the National Council for Teacher Education (1996) are:

1. To develop a critical awareness among teachers and teacher educators regarding the realities of Indian life.
2. To promote such capabilities in them as may be necessary for the realization of national values and goals as enshrined in the constitution of India.
3. To enable them to act as agents of modernization, social change and development, and transmittance of the national and cultural heritage.
4. To cultivate rational thinking and scientific temper.
5. To promote among them the managerial and organizational skills as required in the contemporary Indian educational contexts.
6. To develop among them the capabilities needed for performing their role in dynamic society in order to meet the challenges of community and change.
7. To make them aware of the environmental and ecological problems and enable them to find out suitable solutions.
8. To develop interest/capacity for involvement in community life and draw its resources for the welfare of the school for meaningful education.

9. To develop competencies and skills needed for becoming an effective teacher.
10. To enable them to impart knowledge and reconstruct experiences.
11. To inculcate positive attitudes towards students.
12. To develop the capacities to organize supplementary education activities.
13. To develop interest and skills for undertaking action research/ research.
14. To inculcate among the teachers a sense of value judgement, value commitment and value transmission.
15. To enable teachers to develop aesthetic sense among students.
16. To foster their interest in in-service education/life-long learning.
17. To sensitize pupil towards the promotion of patriotic feelings, national integration, world peace and protection of human rights.
18. To plan and organize for capacity building with a view to enabling them to look into student's need in physical education and helping them in this regard.

PRESENT STATUS OF TEACHER EDUCATION IN INDIA

The contention that teachers are born not made can be true only in a few rare cases. It can also not be contended that training by itself is sure to make a good teacher. But it is generally observed that a teacher with training becomes more mature and confident to perform his task more efficiently. Proper education of the teacher enables them to have a knowledge of how children grow, develop and learn; how they can be taught effectively; and how their inner potentialities can be brought out and developed. Teacher Education enables the future teacher to make optimum use of his time, energy and resources. Education of secondary teachers in India is more than a hundred years old. During this period the concept of training has changed tremendously. In fact the word 'training' itself has been replaced by the word 'education'. Earlier the emphasis was on what were known as the tricks of the trade, i.e., blackboard work, transmission of knowledge, and classroom management. Today the emphasis has been widened to include the entire spectrum of teacher's work in and outside the class and even outside the school.

The teacher education programme should develop the whole personality of the student teacher, i.e., the wholeness of mind and experience. The student teacher should be open-minded. From this open mindedness, sympathy, tolerance, intellectual adaptability, and wide ranging interests will spring out. The training schedule should thus give him time and opportunity to develop a philosophy of life, a map by which he can see himself in relation to other teachers as well as other human beings. The programme should develop a human teacher who possesses such qualities as spontaneity, acceptance, creativity, and self-realization. The programme should give an opportunity to the prospective teacher to relate theory to practice, to search for greater personal understanding of himself and of learning processes of children. Though there is no doubt that methods can never be taught, but methods adopted by other teachers can be suitably and profitably studied. Using such knowledge that is gained, the student teacher will be able to try out various approaches to his work during his later life. The future teacher should possess the necessary skills and competencies, which will make his teaching task easy, useful, and effective.

The prospective teacher should have a sound philosophy of education, knowledge of adequate functioning of psychology, and a dynamic sociological perspective. These and the development of professional skills and competencies should be the basic objective of a teacher education programme.

Glaring defects in the teacher education programmes in India as identified by different educationists are:

1. Artificiality of courses (including theory and practice): The courses adopted are more than a quarter century old. They embody a course content that is not helpful in preparing an effective teacher. The theory courses in particular have no articulation with the practical work and teaching skill requirements. The application of theory to practice leaves enough room for revision and restructuring. The methods of courses are routine and wanting in practical bias. The emerging concepts of educational technology have yet to make an impact on them.

   The practice teaching course as prescribed has assumed the form of a meaningless ritual and its carry over potential in the development of handling instructional problems in actual classroom is very poor (J.C. Aggarwal,1985).

2. Ineffective methods of teaching: Teacher educators in our country are generally averse to innovation and experimentation in the use of methods of teaching. They have shown a remarkable allegiance to the traditional method of instruction – Lecturing and notes dictation. Their acquaintance with modern classroom communication devices is inadequate. In many cases the lecturers are dull, monotonous, and uninspiring. As a consequence of this the student teachers can only talk about the methods but are not competent to use them. The various logical and psychological operations involved in the act of teaching are indicated in a incoherent way (R.A. Sharma, 1989).

3. Less emphasis on development of professional attitude: The entire Teacher Education Programme is so designed that little emphasis is laid on the development of professional attitude that is so important for a sound programme on teacher education. The poor quality of teacher educators coupled with substandard provision of facilities is largely responsible for lack of vigorous and dynamic programmes on the campus. As a result, professional ethics are not developed (B.R. Purkait, 1987).

4. No impact on school practice: The Education Commission (1964-66) has rightly observed that teacher education both at primary and secondary level has become isolated from schools and current developments in school education. The methods of teaching followed in schools, their curricula, and various requirements are totally different from those advocated and implemented in teacher education departments. Not much effort has been put in to bridge the gulf between what school's practice and what teacher education departments strive for.

5. Lack of infrastructure, i.e., laboratory, library and physical education equipment and well-equipped practicing schools.

6. Poor academic background of student teachers: For many the B.Ed course is a stop gap course. Also not much effort has been made to regulate demand and supply of teachers in accordance with various subjects.

7. Absence of empirical research and in service programmes for the development of teacher educators.

The National Policy of Education (NPE) 1986 has emphasized teacher education as a continuous process, its pre-service and in service components being inseparable. The NPE among other things has pointed out the following in respect of teacher education.

(a) Professional commitment and overall competencies of teachers leaves much to be desired.
(b) The quality of pre service education has not improved with recent developments in pedagogical science, but has actually shown signs of deterioration.
(c) Teacher education programmes consist mainly of pre service teacher training with practically no systematic programmes of in service training.

NEEDED ACTION IN TEACHER EDUCATION PROGRAMMES

1. The courses of study both in theory and practice need to be recognized. Pragmatic research should form the basis for reorganizing the course structure in order to reach the goals of education. The ratio of weightage for theory and practical work has to be worked out. A comprehensive job analysis of teaching in schools can necessarily form the framework for recasting courses in teacher education.
2. Each teacher education institute must have basic infrastructural facilities, like a laboratory, a well-equipped library, educational technology equipment, and a well-established demonstration school.
3. The admission procedures need to be regulated so that only those who have an aptitude for teaching are selected.
4. A two-way interaction between the demonstration (practicing) schools and teacher Education colleges is desirable.
5. The intake of student teachers is to be distributed on the basis of demand/supply ratio.
6. Teacher education departments should conduct in-service programmes to use innovative techniques and coordinate activities with other faculties also.

The various activities in the teacher education programmes have to be researched upon and the results may be used to analyze and suggest remedies regarding:

(a) Student Teacher behaviour.
(b) Development of a conceptual framework for a sound theory of instruction.

(c) Skill training and techniques of instruction to be given to student teachers.

(d) Use of innovations—classroom dissemination and teacher training strategies.

In pursuance of the National Policy on Education, District Institutes of Education and Training (DIETs) were established. They were charged with the responsibility of organising pre service and in service education of elementary school teachers. The colleges of teacher education and Institutes of Advanced Studies in Education were given the responsibility of introducing innovations in teacher education programmes at the secondary stage and vocational streams.

INNOVATIONS IN TEACHER EDUCATION

Educationists have advocated the need to revamp the present system of education and to renovate it in such a manner as to fulfil the needs and aspirations of the present society. It has been realized that teachers are the most forceful instruments for bringing about any reform in the present system of education. As a result, they have to be equipped with effective training in order to bring about social changes in the society and help us to establish an egalitarian society that is our objective.

The educational panorama is marked by rapid changes in educational programmes, new technology, and innovations. Education reporting today is very much like snapping a photo of a moving object—by the time the shutter is opened, the picture has changed. With the growth of educational technology as a specialised field, a host of new techniques have been evolved to increase teaching effectiveness.

Programmed instruction/learning was designed to make the educative processes objective, systematic, and purposeful (Skinner, 1954; Green, 1966; Bung, 1967). 'Teaching Machines' based on programmed Instruction and making use of the channels of vision and sound have also been utilized for teachers preparation and evaluation (Holland, 1960; Nordberg, 1965; Dodd, 1968; Richmond, 1970). Microteaching cycles involving teaching, feedback, planning, re-teaching, and re-feedback planning respectively have been used and found to be effective (Allen & Ryan, 1969; Passi, 1971).

'Simulation' as a technique for improving teaching behaviour has also been used in teacher education programmes (Cruick, 1968; Tansey, 1971). Team Teaching based on organizing the total Instructional programmes by inducing the theme of team work into the conduct of instruction has also been practiced (Bijon & Barr, 1966). 'Flanders Interaction Analysis' techniques based on the analysis of teaching behaviour objectively in terms of chains of events and providing feedback has been accepted as an approach for optimizing teacher effectiveness. (Kirk, 1964; Pareek, 1971; Passi, 1975).

Figure 1.2 lists some of the innovations in the field of education, which need to be part and parcel of any teacher education programmes.

Fig. 1.2

Teacher Education: Innovations

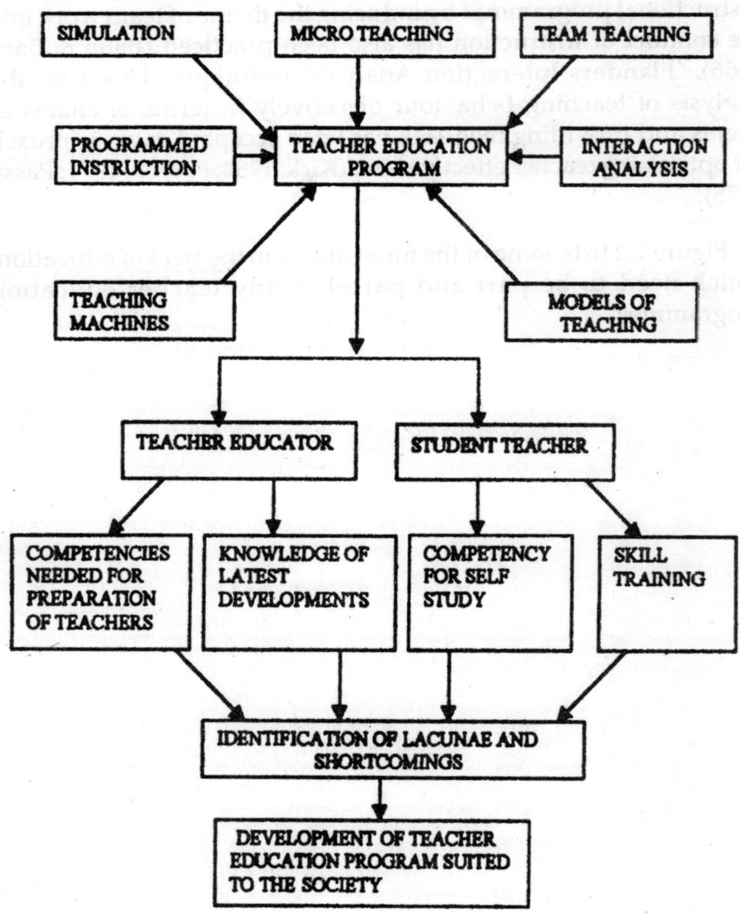

Micro-Teaching

Dwight Allen and Kevin Ryan (1969) define Microteaching as a 'scaled down teaching encounter in class-size and class-time'. Microteaching provides student teachers with a practice setting for instruction in which the normal complexities of classroom are reduced. Micro teaching improves teaching skill, since at the end of each micro teaching session the student teacher discusses his lapses with his supervisor and then repeats his lesson with another small group on the basis of the feedback. This improves his teaching competence. The micro teaching process is shown in Fig. 1.3:

Fig. 1.3

Micro Teaching Cycle

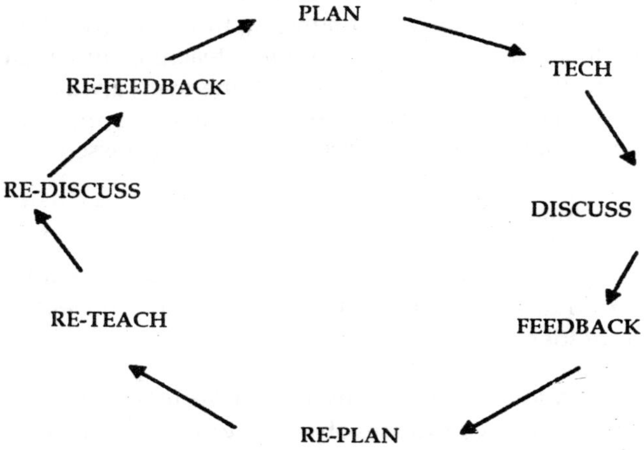

PLAN → TECH → DISCUSS → FEEDBACK → RE-PLAN → RE-TEACH → RE-DISCUSS → RE-FEEDBACK → PLAN

Simulated Social Skill Training (SSST)

It is training in an artificial situation. We can train the students in two ways – (1) on the job (2) off the job. Simulated teaching is off the job teaching. It is done outside the work situation. This system has been defined as a role playing in which the process of teaching is artistically enacted and an effort is made to practice some important skills of communication. The main idea underlying this is to place an individual in a situation which provides spontaneous interaction to see if he can practice producing certain patterns of behaviour. Classroom simulation enables student teachers to come to terms with the demands of a complex skill learning situation without facing the real classroom.

Team Teaching

Team teaching can be considered to be an innovative procedure in organising teaching rather than a method or a technique. It is an instructional design that involves a group of teachers jointly responsible for planning for instruction of a particular course content. The way in which the team of teachers operates constitutes team teaching.

A team teaching programme is based on the teaching objectives, need of the students, their entering behaviour and the techniques proposed to be used in teaching. The size and duration of teaching period vary accordingly. A team teaching programme gives emphasis to joint teamwork in planning, teaching and evaluating rather than the individual teacher. Yet, the team always protects the professional autonomy of each teacher and the opportunity of using the special ability of each teacher is never missed.

Interaction Analysis

Teaching is a system of actions performed to induce learning that is the modification of behaviour in the learner effected through certain activities and experiences.

Interaction analysis is an observation technique for studying classroom interactive processes objectively and systematically. This system consists of a set of procedures, which includes use of different codes and techniques for observing, recording, and analysing classroom interactions between the teacher and the taught. This technique helps in the study of classroom behaviour as teaching progresses and also the teacher behaviour in the class. It can also be used as a feedback for modifying a teacher's behaviour in the classroom.

Programmed Instruction

Programmed Instruction is a highly individualized technique for improving teaching. It is a teaching strategy where learning is effected in each learner in a controlled situation even without the presence of a teacher. This strategy makes use of a variety of teaching aids such as text books, guide books, radio, television, teaching machines and other modern teaching appliances in addition to the teacher.

Programmed Instruction is a method of providing individual instruction to a student giving him the opportunity to learn at his own pace involving himself alone in the learning process. In this mechanism of learning, the learner knows the result of his effort at every step. This method was developed for student learning, but it can also be used as a feedback device for modification of teachers behaviour for effecting improved teaching.

MODELS OF TEACHING

'Models of teaching are really models of learning' (Joyce, Weil with Showers, 1992). This statement in one line is the definition of a model of teaching. The model approach to teaching was first described by Joyce and Weil (1972). Models are highly specific teaching strategies designed to accomplish certain goals. They defined the approach as '...a pattern or plan which can be used to shape a curriculum to select instructional materials and to guide teachers actions'.

R. Lakshmi (1989) while analysing cognitive growth models describes a model as an instructional design which describes the process of specifying and producing particular environmental situations, which causes the student to interact in such a way that a specific change occurs in their behaviour. Elaborating, she says that it is a plan or pattern which is instrumental in shaping the curriculum in relation to different aspects like designing instructional materials or guiding instructions in the classroom.

A model of teaching is merely a tool for thinking about classroom training. It is a set of concepts carefully arranged to explain what teachers and students should do in a classroom, how they should interact, how they should use instructional materials, and how these activities affect what students learn. They help students to acquire information, ideas, skills, values, ways of thinking, and means of expressing themselves.

People who worked in different fields developed the models of teaching. They are based on empirical work, theories, and research. Some of the persons whose theories and researches have contributed to the development of different models are:

- Counsellors and therapists—Erikson, Maslow and Roger.
- Learning theorist—Ausubel, Bruner, and Skinner.
- Development Psychologist—Hunt, Kohlberg, and Piaget.
- Philosophers—Broudy, Dewey and James.

Bruce Joyce and others developed ways of making the theories operational. Thus, each model has a rationale that justifies it and describes what is good and why. Thus models link different skills of teaching to theory.

Families of Models

Bruce Joyce and Marsha Weil (1992) have developed more than twenty models that are grouped on the basis of their chief emphasis, the way they approach educational goals and means. They have organized these models into the following four families.

Fig. 1.4

Schematic Diagram of Families of Models

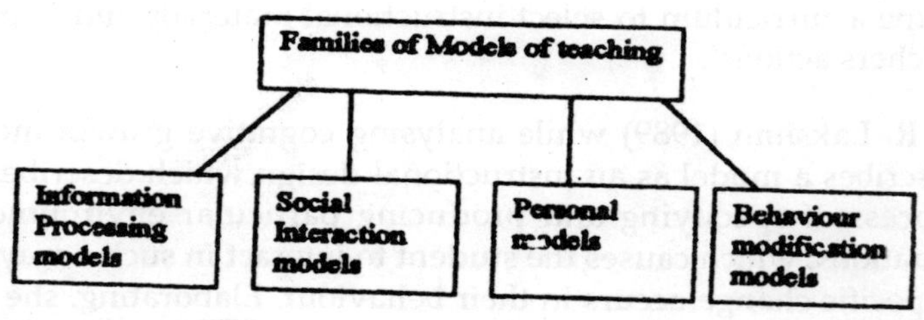

1. Information Processing Models

The models emphasize the ways of enhancing the human beings innate drive to make sense of the world by acquiring and enhancing data, sensing the problems generating solutions for them developing concepts and languages for conveying them.

2. Social Interaction Models

One of the main aims of education is to prepare worthy citizens. The model strives to enhance personal and social life so that a democratic social order prevails in the society. These models combine learning and social living.

3. The Personal Models

Each individual develops a unique personality and looks at the world with his own imagery formed as a product of his experience and position. The personal models of learning begin from the perspective of the selfhood of the individual. They help to shape education so that one can understand oneself better and also understand others around him.

4. The Behaviour Modification Models

The chief guiding factor in building models in this group is that human beings are self correcting communication systems that modify behaviour in response to information about how successfully tasks are navigated.

Fig. 1.5

Schematic Diagram for Models of Teaching

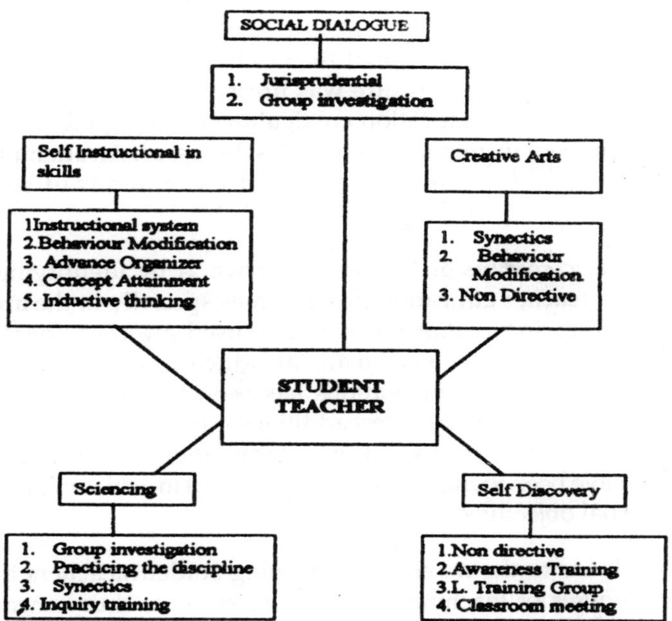

Models in Action

Each model consists of theory and practical training. To translate a theoretical model into practical teaching form, a set of four concepts are used. They are (i) Syntax (ii) Principles of reaction (iii) Social system, and (iv) Support system.

(i) Syntax: Syntax describes the model as a flow of actions. Each model has a distinct flow of sequences or events that are called as 'phases'.

(ii) Principles of reaction: They guide the teacher's response to the learner. They are the rules that the teacher has to follow in response to every action of the learner.

(iii) Social system: It provides a description of student and teacher roles and their inter relationship. It tells us about the norms that are encouraged in the successful implementation of the model.

(iv) Support system: It refers to the additional requirements beyond the usual human skills, capacities, and technical facilities necessary to implement a model.

CONCLUSION

In this chapter, a glimpse of the teacher education scenario in India: past, present and future was presented. The drawbacks in the present teacher education curriculum were highlighted. The need for immediate remedial action was discussed. An attempt was made to suggest needed action based on opinions of several educationists.

The basic conclusion one could arrive at by identifying the lacunae in teacher education programmes specially in the area of science education is that the methods used are traditional and stereotyped. There is a need to introduce new techniques or innovations. A list of innovations has been presented. Of these, models of teaching are the latest additions. Models of teaching have been found to be very useful in improving classroom practices. Models have been identified to be very helpful in achieving various educational objectives.

This leads to the necessity of training student teachers in the use of models of teaching. The present study is thus concerned with satisfying the training needs of student teachers for preparing them to be effective science teachers. In this connection, the first chapter was helpful in identifying the shortcomings in teacher training programmes.

The second chapter describes the various facets of science teaching. It also describes the relevance of Inquiry Training Model in the science education programmes.

Science Education and Inquiry Training Model

INTRODUCTION

A detailed description of the teacher education scenario in India: past and present was presented in the preceding chapter. The lacunae were identified and needed action was discussed. Teacher education programme in science cannot exist in isolation from the school programmes. The needs of the modern scientific and technological society form the basis of school science programme. This in turn becomes indirectly the main objective of the teacher education programme. Any change in teacher education programme in science will have its mirror image in school science programme.

Therefore, it becomes necessary for a proper analysis and understanding of the science education scenario. In this section, an attempt is made to identify the goals and objectives of science education. The methods being used in school science teaching have been briefly discussed. The need for introduction of new techniques in teaching of science has been presented. In this context, a study of the Inquiry Training Model has been taken up in relation to school science teaching and teacher education programme.

GOALS OF SCIENCE EDUCATION

There is no universal agreement regarding the direction in which science instruction has to progress. Science has been regarded as study of nature, of technology, and of the processes of scientific investigation. The fundamental purpose of our school education can be regarded as transmission of culture, accumulated but constantly changing knowledge, skills, and values to the youth of the society. Science is included, principally, because it forms a large and influential part of our culture. In the nineteenth century, religion was the dominant factor and society demanded the inculcation of moral values. The science curriculum at that time was need based. When society needed a reaction against industrialization, the science curriculum stressed emotional and aesthetic goals. The depression of 1930's called upon the schools to teach practical knowledge and the science curriculum emphasis shifted to teaching socially useful skills.

Today, society demands a knowledge of the environmental pollution, hazards of industrialization, the population explosion, etc., and the science curriculum aims to fulfil them.

The goals of science education are

(1) To create a functional understanding of the available generalizations in the body of science. It enables knowing and understanding among students.
(2) To develop coping skills which are essential for making justifiable actions in response to many problems they are to face in future life.
(3) To develop manipulative skills, science education should help students to react rapidly. Science education must have lots of "What... if?", "How?" and "Why?" questions. They must permit the students to check, forecast and alter generalizations.
(4) Only a few students will become practicing scientists. But all of them will reap the benefits of science. Hence they need to be informed about the intellectual and technological base of scientific knowledge.

Thus the minimum result of a science course should be to develop a rational world in which mankind has confidence. Science teaching is not a set of instructions that will help the pupil to commit results to mind. Rather, it should teach him to participate in the process that makes possible the establishment of knowledge. The resultant of science teaching should not be a living library of facts. Science teaching should no doubt expose students to knowledge produced, but in addition, should provide the experience of generating that knowledge.

Thus science teaching is based on these broad aspects:

1. Science is doing not telling: A student should be able to experience science. He can do that only if he is allowed to ask questions on his environment and is given the freedom to seek answers for them. They may have to attempt to find answers by doing some experiments. The teacher should act as a guide and lead the student.
2. To educate students that scientists have no set method: Scientists attack their problems openly and adopt freely any method that promises a solution. A scientist's method can be thoroughly appreciated only by practicing it. Just as a singer learns to sing by practicing singing a pupil learns science only by 'sciencing'.
3. Teach science but not technology: Most children confuse the products of science, which are visible to them as science. They compare the work of the scientist with that of an engineer. They imagine scientists as those who build dams and bombs. They consider them to be constructors of ships and space ships. They are actually not distinguishing between a scientist and a technologist. A scientist tries to describe the behaviour of atomic particles, the nature of bonding between the particles, the effect of splitting atoms and the conditions that lead to forming of an atom, but it is the technologist who builds the atom bomb. When Edison invented the incandescent bulb he was acting not as a scientist but as a technologist. In the same way, when Einstein proposed his 'photo electric effect', he was acting as a scientist.

From the foregoing observations, it can be ascertained that teaching of science emphasizes the teaching of a process, an activity, a system, and an interrogative attitude.

APPROACHES TO SCIENCE TEACHING

There are different approaches to science teaching propounded by different science educators. Anderson, *et al.* (1970) have identified three approaches:

1. Factual approach

2. Conceptual approach
3. Process approach

Factual Approach

The main aim of this approach is to impart the findings of science to students. It helps students to acquire factual information only. It often leads to a poor understanding of the products of science. The most efficient methods of teaching facts are reading, lecturing, recitation, and drill.

Conceptual Approach

In this approach, teaching of major premises/ideas of science is advocated. The major findings are organized into a number of conceptual schemes. Understanding of concepts requires the individual to form schemes. This approach is better than factual approach. The methods that can be used are well-planned lectures and concept attainment model.

Both conceptual and factual approaches are confined to the products of science only.

Process Approach

Science is a dynamic enterprise and an understanding of the process in which, products were formulated. Specific behaviour of students are proposed to be derived from an examination of what a scientist does called the processes of science, i.e., observation, prediction, communication, measurement, classification, and inference.

In this scheme, observation is considered to be the fundamental skill by virtue of its foundation of the hierarchy of skills needed to discover broad knowledge required to conduct inquiry. Measurement, using space/time relations, classification, inference, communication, and prediction form other basic process skills. These are helpful in processing information obtained by observation. The integrated process skills are higher order skills that link processed data with organized conceptual knowledge. These include defining operationally, interpreting data, formulating hypothesis, controlling variables, and experimenting.

Concrete operational thinkers can master basic process skills and the integrated process skills need higher level reasoning abilities among late concrete and formal thinkers.

Theoretically a process approach can give the pupil a valid understanding of the nature of science. He can experience the excitement and frustrations that are a part of science and can understand better its products because he has an awareness of some of the problems of the scientist. Discovery method, Project method, and Inquiry teaching are some of the techniques used to teach process skills.

INQUIRY TEACHING

In a country like India where dogma and superstitions are still prevalent, it becomes imperative of the teacher to stimulate the spirit of inquiry in the minds of the wards he cares for. The inquiry turns scientific when it is systematic. The teacher at any level of educational hierarchy by virtue of his close proximity and association with the developing minds of children has the moral responsibility of inspiring them, guiding them, and, eventually, making them to learn by themselves. A teacher has to educate pupils to develop curiosity, skills to hypothesize, and, most importantly, to test problems and verify the results for himself. Ability to stimulate the spirit of scientific inquiry is undoubtedly a valuable tool in the hands of an intelligent, imaginative, and responsible teacher. He initiates a student to scientific approach and systematic analysis and problem solving, thus enlightening his mind and making him a responsible thinking citizen.

In inquiry approach to science teaching, teaching and learning are 'why' centred. The students are very actively identifying and defining problems, selecting data sources, gathering data, processing the data and in making inferences.

Educationists have variously defined inquiry teaching depending upon their understanding of the method.

An information processing approach to learning stresses the importance of meaningful learning versus rote memorization of content. Elaborating further, Smith (1975) opined that the brain is considered to be an organ whose primary function is to 'actively seek, acquire, select, organize, store, and at appropriate times, retrieve and utilize information about the world'. Inquiry teaching aims at facilitating the brain to perform its functions.

Kuslan and Stone (1969) define inquiry teaching as that teaching by which teachers and children study scientific phenomena with the approach and the spirit of the scientist. Inquiry in operational terms is a learning in which the following instructional characteristics are consistently present:

(i) Scientific processes such as observing, communicating, measuring, testing, predicting, comparing, classifying, experimenting, inferring, analysing, and drawing out induction's are habitually employed by children and teachers.

(ii) Time is unimportant. There is no urgency to complete a topic in order to meet a dead line.

(iii) The answers sought are not known in advance by the children and these answers are not found in textbooks. But textbooks and manuals are chosen because they ask questions and suggest ways of finding answers but do not give answers.

(iv) Children are genuinely interested in finding solutions.

(v) The content of the inquiry is not necessarily related to that which proceeds or follows.

(vi) Teaching and learning are "why" centred. Questions such as "How do we know?", "Are we justified in this assumption?" are characteristic of the Inquiry style.

(vii) A problem of some kind is identified and narrowed until it seems probable that it can be solved by the class.

(viii) Hypotheses are proposed in the class in order to guide the investigation.

(ix) Children take the responsibility of proposing ways of gathering data from controlled experimentation, observation, reading and other pertinent sources.

(x) These proposals for action are co-operatively evaluated. Pertinent assumptions, limitations, and difficulties are identified whenever possible.

(ix) Children investigate in small groups, as a class and as individuals in order to gather data to test the hypotheses.

(xii) Children summarize their data and come to tentative conclusions about the adequacy of their hypotheses. Every effort is made to formulate scientific explanations.

(xiii) Conclusions and explanations are incorporated wherever possible into the various themes of the science.

Thus it can be seen that inquiry teaching is a continuous, sustained and higher order divergent mental activity.

TYPES OF INQUIRY

Undoubtedly the power of natural empirical knowledge is more massive in the present society than ever before. All this knowledge has come in gradual steps that can be identified and dated. The primary principle that has moved mankind is the demand that the basis of any action should be verifiable knowledge. Verification need not necessarily prove to be always true but it underscores the idea that knowledge needs to remain open to public inspection and that is what is inquiry. Every member of our society is born with the right to know and test a philosophy—be that of science or arts.

Inquiry, in general, can be defined as being inquisitive, curious, asking questions or trying to find out for oneself. Inquiry encompasses a broad range of activities performed to explore and search out variables and attributes relevant to discrepant stimuli.

William K. Esler (1973) has listed the following types of inquiry.

(i) Rational Inquiry

A lesson wherein a teacher presents a problem through demonstration, anecdotes, pictures, graphs or tables and conducts a discussion which leads to a generalization is called 'rational inquiry'. The pupils reason their way to gain new insights from the discussion. The teacher does not tell them the conclusions but leads them through questioning to form their own conclusions.

(ii) Discovery Inquiry

The term discovery refers to a situation wherein the teacher presents materials and allows the students to manipulate them. From the tactile experience and verbal interaction that takes place amongst the children and between teacher and children certain conclusions, relationships between variables or generalizations are drawn. In a discovery lesson also the children are not instructed on what to observe. To conclude he presents a summarizing lesson wherein individual children relate their experience and follow the manipulative activities.

(iii) Experimental Inquiry

Experimentation is one of the most stringent forms of inquiry in terms of structure. In experimentation, the students identify a problem, formulate a hypothesis which is an inference concerning possible solutions to the problem. They suggest and carry out procedures for testing their hypothesis. The essential difference between discovery and experimental inquiry is that in the latter all the decisions about how to proceed are decided before any manipulations are made, while in the former manipulations come first followed by a discussion of the results.

PROCESS OF INQUIRY

Process of inquiry refers to 'what children must do to conduct an inquiry'. Specific skills for rational inquiry are ability to observe, classify, and infer relationships. During discovery inquiry the students must be able to observe the interaction, classify the given observations and make a generalization. For conducting experimental inquiry students should be able to hypothesize the effects, control variables and set up experimental conditions. They should be able to observe, measure and communicate data. They should infer and interpret data.

Scientific Inquiry

Scientific inquiry can be broadly defined as a systematic and investigative performance ability which incorporates unrestrained inductive thinking capabilities, after a person has acquired a broad and critical knowledge of the particular subject matter through formal learning processes.

Kenneth D. Peterson (1978) defines inquiry as a systematic and investigative activity with the purpose of discovering and describing relationships among objects and events. He contends that inquiry is characterised by the use of orderly and repeatable processes, reduction of the object of investigation to most simple forms, and use of logical works for explanation and prediction. He lists observing, questioning, experimenting, comparing, inferring, generalizing, communicating, and applying as operations of scientific inquiry.

Discussing about processes of scientific inquiry, John T. Wilson (1976) says that Inquiry begins with stimuli that are contrary to expectations. He characterizes inquiry as a broad range of activities performed to explore and search out variables and attributes relevant to discrepant stimuli. He categorizes the events that invoke inquiry as:

(i) Curious events or observations that cannot be explained by habitual responses.
(ii) Data gaps or failure to find observations that have been predicted by a theory or law.
(iii) Chance observations or events that are recognized by the inquisitive mind that tries to find a rational reasoning for the observations.

Schwab (1963) indicates that by teaching science as inquiry, Americans attitude towards science and scientists would improve immensely. He recognized the fact that a student of the traditional science class falls into a dangerous relativism or cynicism towards science owing to the fact that much of the scientific truth has become obsolete or has been replaced by new theories.

R. Suchman (1961) advanced the idea that inquiry provides a means to individualize and to self paced instruction, so that students are able to learn what is relevant to them. According to Suchman, freedom and responsive environment are necessary for self-directed activity. He contends that the ability to inquire and discover concept autonomously is more important than the attainment of concepts. He opined that through inquiry and the ability to individualize instruction, many of the problems associated with slow or turned off learners would be resolved.

Sund and Trowbridge (1973) emphasize teaching science and inquiry and noted that the essence of inquiry teaching lies in arranging the learning environment to facilitate student-centred instruction. They advocate the need to provide necessary direction and guidance in order that student succeeds in discovering scientific concepts and principles. They recognized the ability of a teacher to ask questions, stimulate, and facilitate creativity and creative thinking as the basic quality for inquiry teaching.

Voss and Brown (1968) emphasized on an inquiry approach in which a student finds out how new knowledge is acquired. They listed creativity, productive thinking, conditioned reflexes, and sufficient knowledge of subject as conditions necessary for a student to take part in inquiry activity.

Similarly, Dress, *et al.* (1960) state that recognition of a problem, collection of relevant data, formulation of hypothesis and drawing conclusions were the chief elements of scientific inquiry.

Saadeh (1969) also believes that inquiry increased intellectual potency and developed critical thinking.

INQUIRY TRAINING MODEL (ITM)

Learning how to learn or development of learning sequences is also an important task of education. Questioning technique is one such learning sequence. Generally, an inquiring mind is curious and it is indicated by the questions asked by it. Sometimes questions may be asked merely out of habit and the questioner may not be bothered to receive the answers properly or evaluate them. Just as the questions of the teachers have to be ordered according to logical sequences, so also the questions of the students must be to a certain extent logically sequenced. Usually, students do not organize their questions in a meaningful way. Their inquiry processes are often of random nature, with only occasional integration of related information. Recognizing the potential value of asking questions in an orderly, purposeful manner, educators have agreed upon the desirability of critical thinking as an important objective. Richard Suchman (1957) was interested in the development of critical inquiry through orderly processes and developed a model of teaching.

The Inquiry Training model as developed by Suchman is classified under the Information Processing models of teaching (Joyce and Weil, 1978). Suchman assumes that human beings are basically curious and problem-solvers by nature. Suchman and his associates tried to analyze the methods employed by creative research personnel, especially physical scientists. As they identified the elements of their inquiry process, they generated the instructional model called Inquiry Training Model (Mani, R.S., 1985).

Suchman and his associates (1957) found out the conditions that are essential to create inquiry. They are as follows:

1. Children need some kind of problem stimulus and preferably though not necessarily, one that is discrepant to the schema of conceptual systems of the child, i.e., one that cannot be readily assimilated.
2. Children need condition of freedom. Suchman has broken down freedom into two parts: (i) External freedom—physical freedom to reach out for desired data and information and to acquire it at any rate in any sequence the child wants. (ii) Internal freedom—Autonomy in their actions to think independently.
3. Children need responsive environment. When a child reaches out for data he must not return empty handed. He must be in a position to procure some information, otherwise it will lead to disappointment and disinterest.

Objectives of Inquiry Training Model

B.K. Passi, *et al.*, have listed the following as the objectives of Inquiry Training Model:

1. To develop scientific process skills—i.e., observing, collecting and organising data, identifying and controlling variables, formulating, and testing hypothesis, explanation and inferring among students.
2. To develop among students the strategies for creative inquiry.
3. To develop among students an independence or autonomy in learning.
4. To develop among students the ability to tolerate ambiguity.
5. To make students realize that all knowledge is tentative.
6. To develop verbal expressiveness among students.

Inquiry Training as a Model of Teaching

Syntax, principles of reaction, social system and support system are the four components of ITM as a model of teaching.

Syntax for ITM: It is the plan of action that a teacher has to follow while using ITM in the classroom. It is divided into five phases.

Phase 1: Encounter with the problem: In this phase the teacher explains the rules of the model and presents a puzzling or problem situation.

Phase 2: Data gathering – Verification

Phase 3: Data gathering – Experimentation

In phase 2 and 3 students have to gather data for analysis, verification and experimentation. The students are required to ask series of questions such that the teacher can answer by only 'yes' or 'no'. There are three distinct steps in the data gathering process:

(i) Verifying the nature of objects, conditions and properties and occurrence of event.
(ii) Isolating the irrelevant variables and conditions through experimentation could be of two-type (a) verbal and (b) manipulative.
(iii) Hypothesizing and testing causal relationships through experimentation.

Phase 4: Formulation of an Explanation: In this phase the students try to formulate an explanation on the basis of the data gathered in Phases 2 and 3.

According to Suchman theory building takes place at four levels:

(a) Simple linear causation.
(b) Theories of properties.
(c) Analysis.
(d) Application of a generalization.

Phase 5: Analysis of Inquiry Process: In this phase the students analyze their patterns of thinking. They identify the questions that were useful in analysing data and those that were irrelevant.

Principles of Reaction of ITM

In this model the most important reactions of the teacher takes place during the second and third phases. In the second phase, the task of the teacher is to help the students to inquire but not to do the inquiry for them. Many a time students may ask questions that cannot be answered with a 'yes' or 'no'. In such situations, the teacher must ask the students to rephrase their questions so that their attempt to collect data progresses smoothly. The teacher can if necessary keep the ball of inquiry rolling by making new information available to the group and focus on a particular problem even by raising questions.

Social System of ITM

'This model is based on the assumption that team approach is better than individual approach. The social system here is cooperation. The teacher and students participate as equals where ideas are concerned. Teacher acts as a facilitator to conduct the students in their pursuit of an explanation to the discrepant event.

(a) **Teacher's Role**: The teacher performs a large number of roles in this model. He selects the problem situation, acts as a referee in the inquiry, responds to the students queries, probes with necessary information, helps beginners to focus on inquiry process, facilitates discussion of the problem situation among students, acts as a recorder, keeps track of Inquiry by recording theories and types of questions on the black board, and helps students to arrive at explanations.

(b) **Student's role**: Students play an active role in this model. They find out the discrepancy from the problem and try to account for it. They collect data by asking pinpointed questions that can be answered by a 'yes' or 'no'. They logically arrange data gathered and try to put forward suitable explanations. They finally suggest analogies and generalize the theory.

(c) **Classroom procedure**: This model emphasizes group activity. The students are given the freedom to interact among themselves. They can arrange their places at their will. They can consult the library, perform experiments or use any related books. The model requires an open classroom climate where the teacher acts as an instructional manager and monitor.

Support System of ITM

The main requirements of this model are a set of discrepant events, teacher's knowledge about the inquiry process and resource material related to the problem.

Instructional and Nurturant Effects of ITM

Joyce and Weil (1992) have advocated that ITM has two effects—Instructional effects and Nurturant effects. Given below is the diagrammatic representation of the effects of Inquiry Training Model (Fig. 2.1):

Fig. 2.1

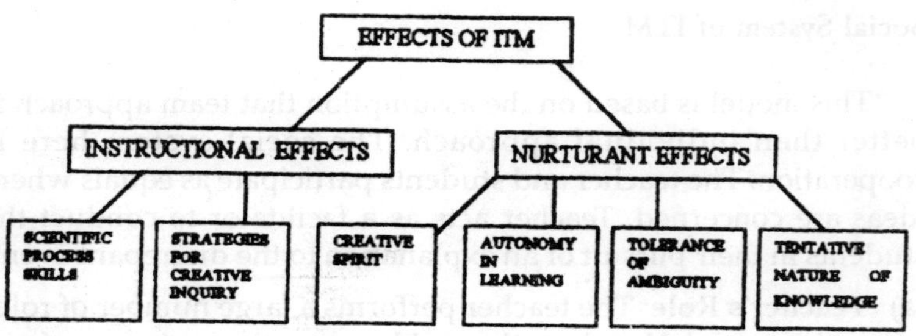

To facilitate the climate of Inquiry, Suchman (1957) has formulated seven principles.

1. Ensuring that questions are so phrased that they can be answered by a 'yes' or 'no'.
2. Asking students to rephrase invalid questions.
3. Pointing out invalidated statements.
4. Using the language of the inquiry process—for instance, identifying students' questions—theories and inviting testing (experimenting).
5. Neither approving nor rejecting students theories.
6. Pressing students for clearer statements of theories and more support for generalizations.
7. Encouraging interactions among students.

To formulate the climate of inquiry Suchman (1957) provided six rules for inquiry sessions:

1. The questions should be phrased in such a way that they can be answered 'yes' or 'no'.
2. 'Once called upon, a student may ask as many questions as he or she wishes before yielding the floor.
3. The teacher does not answer 'yes' or 'no' to statements or theories or to questions that attempt to obtain the teachers

approval of a theory. Hence the teacher has to be very cautious at this stage.

4. Any student can test any theory at any time. The students should argue the merits of one another's theories and feel free to test all the theories that have been advanced.
5. Anytime the students feel a need to confer with one another without the teachers presence, they should be free to call a conference.
6. Inquiries should be able to work with experimental kits, books or resource books at any time.

NEED/ RATIONALE OF THE STUDY

In the preceding sections, a panoramic view of the teacher education and school science education scenario was presented. There is an absolute necessity to bring about reforms in teacher education programmes to suit the present day needs of schools and society. Both school teaching and teacher education programmes have been amply discussed in the preceding sections. In this section an attempt is made to present the need/ rationale of the study, objectives of the study, and limitations of the study undertaken by the investigator.

We cannot discuss science teacher education as a separate entity from science education. In this connection, Brunkhorst *et al.* (1993) says that: "Science teacher education is now recognized as the pivotal point in the reform of science education...no longer can we view science teacher preparation as discrete and separate from science teacher enhancement."

Trumbull and Kerr (1993) recognize the need for improvement of Pre college science teaching and assert that the only way to do so is to improve preparation of science teachers.

Three questions can be addressed towards the act of teaching. They are What? Why?, and How? of teaching. The 'What' of teaching essentially deals with the content to be taught. New topics are being added, obsolete ones are removed, insufficient aspects are recast and continuous revision of facts to be taught is being done in all subject domains. This aspect has been discussed and researched upon extensively.

The 'Why' of teaching concerns itself with the rationale of teaching a particular content. It is a reasoning to justify the inclusion of 'What' of teaching. Even this aspect has been given enough thought by educationists. What and why are thus connected with the 'products' of teaching.

The 'How' of teaching is necessarily concerned with the process of teaching. It is now being recognized as an important component of teaching. Educationists are according recognition to it of late.

To teach successfully one must plan successfully. Successful planning requires an understanding of how to facilitate a positive learning experience. The learner autonomy and individual differences have to be catered to. This requires a judgment on the part of a teacher as to which technique has to be adopted. A teacher can in fact control the teaching effectiveness of his classroom. A passive teacher simply relies on the same old traditional techniques day after day. He confines himself to the traditional techniques and is not prepared to accept change.

Schnur and Golby (1995) assert that "If future teachers are not to become robotic clones of the present teachers and if future schools are to be mere replicas of present schools, teacher education must develop its own independence of thought and inquiry."

An active teacher in comparison is one who is dynamic and changes his tactics as and when the situation demands. If we need to develop active teachers, then we have to instil in student teachers an attitude of experimentation. But, Kamlesh Choudhary (1986) has summarized the general state of teacher education programmes. He comments that, "The present teacher education programmes in India rely heavily on training students in a few basic teaching skills through micro teaching under simulation and peer practices. They are then asked to teach in schools according to Herbartian steps. Whether teaching facts, principles, concepts or problems the same method is followed. Apart from a lack of variety in teaching, the assumption that there is one best method of teaching is preposterous."

A student teacher has to be trained in using a variety of techniques in order to enable him to actively use them in his practice later. The success or failure of any strategy adopted depends on a number of factors:

(i) Appropriateness of technique
(ii) Utility of technique
(iii) Implementation of technique, and
(iv) Receptiveness of learner.

The technique chosen should be relevant to the topic to be taught. It should lead to the fulfilment of the objectives of the lesson. A technique should not be used only for the sake of introducing a new environment. It should serve a purpose. Certain strategies require the adaptation of specific rules and also need a proper classroom climate. The teacher has to be familiar with all the procedures and rules. The students must also be aware of the special requirements of the technique.

Thus the rationale of choosing of one strategy over another depends upon objectives, content, learner needs, learning principles, instructional resources, teaching competencies, and climate in the school.

Ronald J. Bonnsletter (1992) advocates the necessity of a variety in teaching strategies. He identifies different learning styles among students. For example, in the US, recent studies suggest that 10-20% are Oral learners, 20–30% are Visual learners and 30% are Kinesthetic. Thus students differ dramatically in the ways they learn and certain students learn only when material is presented through their learning style. In the case of US students, at least 50 % of them learn by doing. Hence, it is absolutely necessary for a teacher to be aware of different learning styles of his pupils. In addition, he should develop his teaching styles to suit learner styles. To do so a teacher should have a knowledge of various techniques of teaching.

Teaching is considered to be more than mere imparting knowledge and communication of facts. It is considered to be a process of helping learners to learn. It should be a path for individuals to acquire skills and develop their own inherent competencies. Teaching should facilitate individual development. A teacher should act as an agent who provides facilities for shaping behaviour of students.

This leads us to the preparation of teachers or teacher education. It is the responsibility of the teacher educators to impart the required skills. The teacher education programme should be one that satisfies the needs of modern day schools. The programme should cater to both the average as well as creative teachers. The skill training should be designed suitable to the highly intellectual and the average intelligence student teachers also. The programme should lead to the assimilation and internalization of ideas, facts, and skills. By the completion of the programme, the student teacher must be conversant of the latest innovations. He should have reviewed the latest researches and be aware of the new techniques. He should have a theoretical understanding of the innovation. He must possess the required skills to implement it. He should have a favourable reaction and attitude towards innovation:

Figure 2.2 is a diagrammatic representation of various functions of a teacher:

Fig. 2.2

Functions of a Teacher

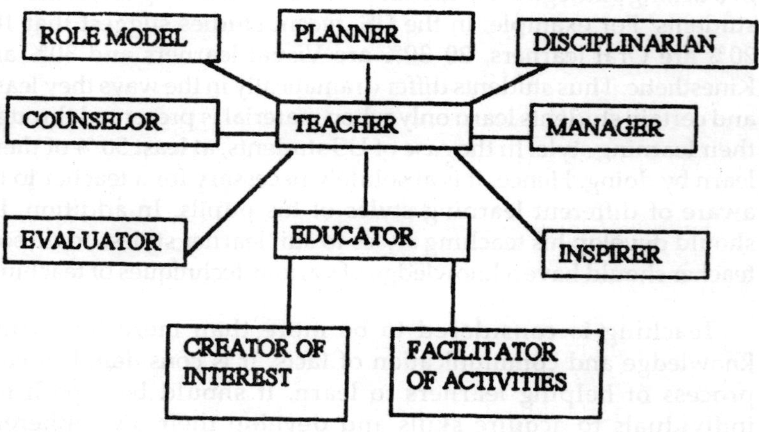

In order to perform all the above-mentioned roles of teacher he needs to have competencies suitable for the diverse roles. The teacher styles have to be developed in the training stage. To perform these multifaceted roles, training in 'models of teaching' could be the ultimate solution. Models of teaching are prescriptive teaching strategies. They are different from the other general approaches to teaching since they are designed to achieve specific instructional objectives whereas general approaches are applicable to all teaching situations. Models were designed to provide guidelines for designing educational objectives, activities, and environments.

Models present powerful cognitive and social tasks to their students and teach the students to make productive use of them. The main purpose of the models is to increase aptitude to learn. Models try to develop learning capabilities in order to make them powerful learners. The models help in maintaining favourable classroom climate since most of them require active participation of students. The diversion of students' minds and energies towards unnecessary activities will be minimized. The students are encouraged to ask questions, discover, role play or engage in activities which they normally would not do in regular classes. It develops in them a sense of participation and cooperation.

Models act as a motivating factor to the teachers also. It encourages the teachers, since the students are actively responding. It enables him to provide a new outlook to his teaching. The common refrain of many teachers is boredom. After a few initial years, the teacher becomes an expert lecturer and does not find a charm in teaching. He finds his job dull and monotonous. Use of models of teaching could probably help to dismiss such words as boredom, dull, monotonous, etc., from a teacher's dictionary. The choice of varied techniques keeps him active in planning and implementation. It will make him to develop a healthy attitude towards his profession and leads to job satisfaction.

This being the multifaceted use of 'models of teaching' the need of the hour is their introduction in classrooms. The requirement is that of trained manpower. There is a need to identify training schedules to fit into existing training programmes.

As a beginning this study was undertaken on Inquiry Training Model (ITM). ITM was developed by Richard Suchman to teach students a process of investigation. Based on the principles of scientific method, the study attempts to teach students some of the skills and procedures of scholarly scientific inquiry. It helps students to develop cognitive skills of searching and processing data. Through application of logic it helps him to learn to inquire independently and productively. This approach enables students to build concepts through the analysis of concrete episodes and discovery of relationships between variables. Students have a natural motivation to inquire. All that the teacher needs to do is to select examples that have sufficiently surprising outcomes, to make it difficult to the students to remain indifferent to it.

Inquiry skill training is one of the chief aims of science teaching. The knowledge of ITM is an absolute necessity for every prospective teacher since ITM is concerned with development of Inquiry skills. Keith Postlethwaite (1989) makes this fact clear. He opines that teaching and teacher education can progress only through inquiry techniques. He says knowledge of subject matter that a student teacher is to teach though necessary can never be a sufficient preparation for the task of teaching. He feels that teachers must be active investigators of their own teaching and inquiry based teaching must begin with the induction of student teacher into teaching. This he opines will enable the student teachers to move from simple competence to professional excellence.

Recognizing the fact that Inquiry Training Model can be a valuable tool in a beginning teachers repertoire, Paul, Eggen *et al.* (1981) have listed the following advantages of training in Inquiry strategies for pre service teachers :

(i) Inquiry strategy provides the teacher with means of teaching students problem solving.
(ii) Inquiry strategies provide alternate means of teaching content to students who may be already saturated with teacher oriented expository techniques. Inquiry activities can be motivating alternatives to other approaches since students are actively involved in each of the phases.
(iii) Inquiry strategy provides them with a model to follow in order to solve problems in other areas of their lives in addition to solving classroom problems.

The stages in the inquiry model provides student teachers with practice in information gathering and analysis skills which have a wide application in other facets of life.

Thus, the various facts presented in the preceding pages have amply demonstrated the need for introduction of innovations in teacher education programmes. This leads to the immediate requirements of training needs and training strategies with regard to student teachers. In order to accomplish the above needs, the requirement is that of teacher educators who have adequate knowledge and skills.

RESEARCH QUESTIONS

Thus, three important Research Questions that were raised in the present study are:

Question No. 1: Are the teacher educators willing to implement innovations (models of teaching)?

Question No. 2: What would be the training strategy that is suitable to train student teachers to use ITM?

Question No. 3: What would be the response of the student teachers—the ultimate beneficiaries to the training provided in ITM?

Figure 2.3 is a diagrammatic representation of the factors that effect Implementation of Innovations:

Fig. 2.3

Implementation of Innovations

DURATION OF TRAINING SCHEDULE

TRAINING SCHEDULE

TYPE OF TRAINING SCHEDULE

INSTITUTIONAL SUPPORT

SUCCESSFUL IMPLEMENTATION OF INNOVATION

1. CONVENTIONAL APPROACH
2. EDUCATIONALTECHNOLOGY APPROACH
3. SMALL GROUP APPROACH
4. MODULAR APPROACH

INNOVATIVE READINESS

TEACHER EDUCATOR CHARACTERISTICS

STUDENT TEACHER CHARACTERISTICS

1. ATTITUDE TOWARDS INNOVA-TIONS
2. WILLINGNESS TO IMPLEMENT
3. APITITUDE TO ACCEPT CHANGE
4. PEDAGOGICAL DEVICES USED
5. RESEARCH ORIENTATION.

1. ATTITUDE TOWARDS INNOVA-TIONS
2. WILLINGNESS TO IMPLEMENT
3. APITITUDE TO TRY OUT NEW CONCEPTS
4. RESEARCH ORIENTATION.

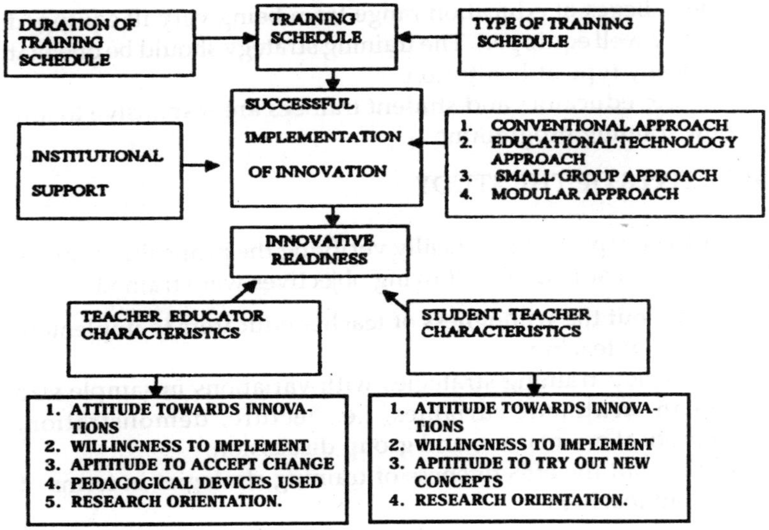

The present study is designed to evolve teaching strategies to train graduate student teachers in the use of Inquiry Training Model of teaching physics. The relative effectiveness of different training strategies in terms of (a) theoretical understanding, (b) reaction towards the model and (c) willingness to implement the model was studied. The training strategies are three large group approaches and three small group approaches. The training schedules are variations in theoretical orientation, lecture—demonstration and discussion.

WORKING ASSUMPTIONS OF THE STUDY

Working Assumptions of the study are:

1. Teacher Education needs continuous revision. The syllabus and curriculum need to be updated periodically.
2. Teacher Education Programmes require innovative practices to make it suitable for present day needs.
3. Innovations—Training strategies have to be devised keeping teacher-pupil ratio in view, i.e., Teacher-pupil ratio is generally 1: 50 or more in science methods class.
4. Teacher education programmes are of very short duration (10 months-1year) and are hence crammed for time. Therefore the training approaches should be of very short duration and yet be in a position to deliver goods.
5. The colleges of education range from being very ill equipped to very well equipped. The training strategy should be one that suits any type of Institution.
6. Teacher educators and student trainees are responsive to any new training programme.

OBJECTIVES OF THE STUDY

For the purpose of practically verifying the propositions in the chosen area of study, the following objectives were framed:

1. To find out the willingness of teacher educators to implement models of teaching.
2. To develop training strategies with variations in sample size and in treatment variables, i.e., lecture, demonstration, theoretical orientation, and group discussion.
3. To find out the effectiveness of training strategies in terms of student teachers.

(i) Theoretical understanding of ITM
(ii) Attitude towards ITM
(iii) Willingness to implement ITM

LIMITATIONS OF THE STUDY

1. This was a study attempting to contribute to the area of teacher education curriculum. It was an attempt at finding out how an innovation introduced in the teacher education programme would be viewed by teacher educators and how the student teachers would respond to the innovation training strategy. The investigator was aware of the fact that a variety of innovations were possible in the science teacher education curriculum and the innovation chosen for this study was only a small component of the various possibilities.
2. The working environment in the various colleges of education was receptive and co-operative. The current teacher education programme was so tightly scheduled that the investigator found it difficult to implement a well planned experimental design.
3. The investigator chose a 'Simple Methods Experiment' design to study the effects of training strategies.
4. English and Telugu translations of the tools were used to assess the student teachers response to the training imparted.
5. The investigation was confined to teacher educators and student teachers only. The implementation of ITM during practice teaching by student teachers after undergoing training in ITM was not included in the purview of the study.
6. The administrative and time constraints placed a limitation on the study where a comparative study of the post-training effects only was undertaken.
7. The invèstigator did not participate in the training schedules to prevent experimental bias and to maintain objectivity of the study. The concerned teacher educators in the colleges' chosen were themselves involved in the training programme. No attempts were made to equate professional competence of different teacher educators who participated in the investigation.

Thus the study undertaken is titled as

A Study of the Inquiry Training Model in Science Teacher Education Programme'

3

Related Research

INTRODUCTION

Research in Education, as in other fields, is an endeavour to reach out for knowledge. It is not a search that yields infallible truths, but it is a search that provides knowledge for the solution of problems in the field of education. Research takes the advantage of the knowledge, which has accumulated in the past as a result of constant human endeavour. Research can never be undertaken in isolation of the work that has already been done on the problems that are directly or indirectly related to the study proposed by the researcher. Therefore, careful reviews of the research journals, books, dissertations, theses and other sources of information on the problem are very essential for any research.

The present study is formulated to design and evaluate training strategies to train pre-service student teachers (B.Ed.) to use Suchman's Inquiry Training Model. Therefore, the research studies related directly or indirectly are reviewed in this chapter.

In India, during the last four decades efforts have been made to study the classroom behaviour of teachers through Flander's Interaction Analysis Category System which equips them to change their teaching behaviour so that development of pupils can be brought about. Efforts were also made to identify teaching skills for teaching different subjects. Also the micro teaching technique was researched for improving upon general teaching and teaching skills. Another group of researchers tried to find out the teaching patterns that are conducive for developing cognitive and affective behaviour. It is generally agreed that the objectives to be achieved through the teaching-learning process are multi-dimensional in nature. It is also felt that a particular method or technique may not be appropriate for achieving the multi-dimensional objectives. This led researchers to explore various methods in an integrated fashion that resulted in the development of new instructional strategies. The greatest emphasis was on development of the cognitive domain. All these efforts did little for achieving the all round development of the personality of the child. In other words cognitive, affective and psychomotor behaviour must be developed in a balanced and integrated fashion. Models of teaching have great potentiality for achieving this goal of education. Joyce and Wiel (1980) developed more than 20 models that were grouped on the basis of their chief emphasis – the way they approached educational goals and means. They have classified models into 4 families. They are:

(1) Information Processing models.
(2) Social Interaction models.
(3) Personal models.
(4) Behaviour Modification models.

Relating to models of teaching Chitriv at Nagpur completed the first study at Ph.D. level (in India) in 1983, while at M.Ed. level Buddhisagar at Indore conducted the first study. These studies relate to training of teacher educators and student teachers in models of teaching.

The following are the studies, in which models of teaching have been used (Fourth Survey of Research in Education in India):

1. Advance Organizer Model (Buddhisagar 1979, Patania 1980, Malik 1985, Rajoriya 1986, Panda 1986, Senapati 1986).
2. Inquiry Training Model (Katyal 1985, Dubey 1986)
3. Concept Attainment Model (Kumaria 1985, Pani 1985, Das 1986, Behari 1986, Gangrade 1986)
4. Jurisprudential Inquiry Model (Tiwari 1986)
5. Non Directive Model (Sahani 1986)

While comparing the Concept Attainment Model and Advance Organizer Model with traditional methods in terms of performance and concept knowledge test, Chitriv (1983) found that the Advance Organizer as well as Concept Attainment Model were significantly superior to traditional method. Advance Organizer Model was superior to Concept Attainment Model for teaching mathematical concepts to XI grade students.

Prose passage type and pictorial type advance organizers facilitated retention of life science subject matter even after four weeks (Ghosh 1986). Ghosh also observed that instructional strategy with a pictorial type of advance organizer was found to be better than prose passage type of advance organizer.

Pandey (1980) reported that both Advance Organizer and Inquiry Training Model were significantly superior to the traditional methods in terms of pupil achievement whereas all methods were equally effective in terms of pupils attitude towards social studies.

The Concept Attainment Model and Biological Science Inquiry Model were found to be significantly superior to conventional teaching in terms of Class VIII pupils achievement (Sushma 1989). The Concept Attainment Model and Inductive Thinking Model were found to be superior to traditional method in terms of concept attainment and retention.

STUDIES RELATED TO INQUIRY TEACHING IN SCHOOLS

1. The purpose of the study conducted by Nemar Medhat Ahmed (1979) was to investigate quantitatively the overall change in the six instructional outcomes that may be attributed to the teaching of Biology as inquiry. The outcome variables were achievement, science process skills, critical thinking, laboratory skills, attitudes towards science and scientists and interest in science. The effectiveness of the inquiry approach in teaching biology was determined by calculating "effect sizes" for the different outcome variables for each study in a common matrix for all studies. The result was an estimate of how different the inquiry group was from the control group across all collected studies. The coded information of each study including the values of the effect sizes that were calculated for each outcome variable contributed the database for the statistical analysis. A special exploratory data analysis technique

was also used to provide more accurate estimation of the average effect sizes of the Inquiry approach.

The result revealed a definite superiority in favour of teaching biology as inquiry over the traditional approach in helping students development of the instructional (objective) outcomes. Students taught by inquiry mode of instruction improved their science process skills, scientific attitudes, critical thinking, achievement and laboratory skills more than students taught by traditional approach.

2. Al-Khayyat and Abdul Kareem. A. (1980) conducted an experimental study comparing the effects of the inquiry method and the traditional method for teaching social studies in two secondary schools for boys. The main purpose of this study was to compare the effectiveness of inquiry method and traditional method of teaching history on the achievements, attitude and critical thinking ability of the students. The basic design chosen for the experiment was adopted from an experimental design referred to as the Non-randomized control group pre-test/post-test design by Van Dalen and Meyer (1973). Six classes from two secondary schools for boys were involved in the study and there were 25 students in each class. Three history teachers were involved, each teaching one class by the inquiry teaching method and a second class by the traditional method. The students' raw scores on the following instruments measured the determination of the effectiveness: 1. The Watson-Glasser Critical Thinking Appraisal administered as pre and post tests. 2. An attitude test towards history developed by the investigator and administered as pre and post tests. 3. An achievement test, developed by the teachers was administered only as a post-test.

The result of the pre-tests showed that the students in the six classes of both inquiry and traditional groups possessed the same level of critical thinking and attitude towards history. Once the equivalence was established the experiment was administered for 4 weeks.

The results indicated that the inquiry second year students in the two schools performed significantly better than the traditional second year students in the same schools on the achievement test and Watson Glaser Critical Thinking Appraisal. There was no significant difference in the attitude of the students in both the schools.

3. The purpose of the study by Johnston, Susanne Craig (1980) was:

(1) To determine if there was a correlation between achievement scores in science and scores on formal operations test in Junior High School students
(2) To find evidence indicating whether a higher level of operational thought was related to achievement of higher scores in inquiry based science than in non-inquiry based science in Junior High School.

All of the four hundred students of a Rural Junior High School were tested within the shorthand longest test to determine their operational level. Classifying non-procedural teacher and students teaching using Bloom's taxonomy each science section was ranked as inquiry or non-inquiry. A Pearson product moment correlation was run between the operational scores obtained from the longest test and yearly average science grades, between science achievement scores from the Differential Aptitude Test and grades and between operation scores and science achievement scores.

The results indicated that the 52% of the population was found to be formal operational. Scheffe's Test run on the ANOVA indicated that:

i. There was a significant difference between students with high grades, achievement scores and operational level in inquiry classes and students with low grades, achievement scores and operational levels in non-inquiry classes.
ii. There was a significant difference between students with low grades, achievement scores, and operational levels in inquiry classes and students with high grades, achievement and operational levels in non-inquiry classes.
iii. There was a significant difference between students with low grades, achievement and operational levels in inquiry classes and students with high grades, achievement and operational levels in non-inquiry classes.

4. Mc.Adams and William Dossett (1980) attempted to compare structured and inquiry instructional approaches in affecting eight grade students understanding of and response to the persuasive

language usage in the media. The structured approach was conducted by having students role-play mass communicators, after being instructed with mini-lectures based on concepts from Sociology and Social Psychology that dealt with the double speak committee concerns. The inquiry approach was based on Neil Postman's teaching: A Subversive Activity. Responses were sought from the students in both the cognitive and affective domains. The results showed that neither the structured instructional approach nor the inquiry instructional approach was effective in increasing awareness or affecting behavioural patterns of the students.

5. Maria Carl (1981) conducted an experimental study to evaluate the effectiveness of the use of Inquiry instruction to foster creativity in intermediate grade students. The aim of this study was to determine the effect of Inquiry science instruction in fostering creativity in 4th, 5th and 6th grade students.

The tools used were (1) Inquiry profile instrument, and (2) Verbal and Figural test of the Torrance test of creative thinking. For analysis of data, two way analysis of variance with a covariant was run using the general linear model.

The findings of the study indicated that there was no significant difference between the scores of the verbal test for the 4th grade treatment and control subjects. 5th and 6th grade treatment subjects scored significantly higher on the verbal test than the control group. No significant difference was observed between the scores of the two groups on the figural test.

6. Sunita Katiyal (1985) investigated the effect of Inquiry Training Model on learning outcomes in comparison to traditional teaching. The main aims and objectives of this study were to find out the students' reactions about the new approach, that is, "Inquiry Training Approach and Traditional Teaching". The study was carried out in two schools on the students of seventh class.

The achievement scores of students of experimental group were significantly higher than the achievement scores of the students of control group after experimentation. This proved the usefulness of Inquiry Training approach for increasing the achievement of students than the traditional approach students also showed highly favourable reaction towards this new approach.

7. Alpana Dubey (1986) studied the efficacy of inquiry training in learning outcomes. The learning outcomes of the students taught by inquiry training approach was significantly higher even at 0.01 level in comparison to the mean learning outcome of the students of control group taught by traditional approach. One of the minor aims of her study was to determine the creativity of the students. The analysis was done in verbal and non-verbal creativity. In verbal creativity the mean scores of experimental group were higher than the mean scores of control group in all areas such as fluency, flexibility and originality total verbal creativity. But the difference was not significant even at 0.05 level. The relationship of fluency, flexibility and total verbal creativity with achievement was low.

8. The study by Black and Daniel Hug (1981) was designed to investigate the difference between using inquiry and the expository methods for the increase of critical thinking skills of high school senior students. Four hypotheses were tested for comparing the mean scores of the inquiry and non-inquiry students for significant differences on the pre-test and post-test at levels of composite scores, knowledge acquisition, comprehension, ability to analyze and synthesize and the ability to evaluate information. Data were gathered through the use of an instrument the Sequential Test of Educational Progress; Social Studies (1979). The step III social studies test was used as both the pre-test and post-test for measuring the difference between the mean scores of the senior high school students using the inquiry method and repository method. Treatment was for six weeks. Data was analysed at the 0.05 level of significance by using the 't' test for independent means and for related means.

The results showed that although there were no significant difference between the inquiry and expository groups at any level on the post test the inquiry group had greater mean score gains. Although there were no significant difference between the means of inquiry students on pre and post test, the inquiry students registered more gains at each level. There were no significant differences between the mean scores of the expository students on the pre-test and pro-test.

9. The study conducted by Chermart, K. (1981) aimed at finding the relationship between Inquiry teaching process and students achievement in Advanced Placement American history classes.

The purpose of the study was to find out the relationship between methods of social studies and development of inquiry skills among students. The tests used were (1) Cornegie Skill Test (CST), (2) Advanced Placement Multiple Choice section and Advanced Placement Document based questions, (3) Written exercise in historical interpretation, and (4) Teacher checklist on the model was developed by the researcher to differentiate those instruction which emphasize direct discovery method.

Pearson's product moment correlation was applied in the analysis of data collected to test the hypotheses.

The result confirmed Bruners theory that inquiry mode of instruction could be used for developing analytical skills among students. Those students who received more inquiry instruction scored significantly higher on the Advanced placement which were document based questions in comparison to those who received less inquiry instruction. No significant correlation was found between the inquiry teaching process and students performance and multiple choice questions. The correlation between teacher attitudes towards inquiry teaching and the implementation of inquiry method in the classroom was not significant.

10. The study by Leonilla Menezes (1989) was designed to investigate the effect of Inquiry teaching on develcpment of Inquiry skills, Verbal creativity and Achievement in History of class VI students of a higher primary school. An equivalent group post-test experimental design was adopted to evaluate the inquiry training strategy and the conventional method of teaching.

The findings were that inquiry training strategy was more effective in developing inquiry skills than conventional method. There was no significant relationship between student's intelligence and mastery of inquiry skills. The creativity of students taught by inquiry training approach was found to be better. Also the students achievement taught by inquiry approach was better than the students taught by conventional approach.

The study by Jyoti R. Ugru (1990) attempted to see the effect of inquiry training strategy on process skills and achievement on biology. The sample of the study was 56 students of class VIII of Demonstration School, RIE, Mysore. Students were assigned to the experimental and control group using matching technique based on percentile scores obtained in Raven Progressive Matrices test. The control group was taught by the conventional method and the experimental group was taught by inquiry approach. The instruction was spread over 10 days. The tools used were the "process skill test" and "achievement test in Biology".

The major findings were

(1) There was no significant difference between the means of gain scores in process skills in Biology of experimental and control groups.
(2) There was a significant sex difference between means of gain scores in process skill in Biology, of experimental group in prediction and inference, i.e., girls were better than boys.
(3) There was no significant difference between the students of different intellectual levels in experimental and control groups in process skills in Biology.
(4) There was a significant difference between the means of gain scores in achievement in Biology with respect to all objectives and total scores of experimental and control groups.

12. A study conducted by Sivakumar and Prema (1997) in the Department of Education at Alagappa University, Karaikudi, India was aimed at finding out the effectiveness of Suchman's Inquiry Training Model in learning Biology.

The study was conducted on 200 students of IX standard of a Secondary School at Karaikudi. They compared the effectiveness of students taught through ITM and those taught through conventional teaching of Biology.

The results indicated that training in ITM improves the achievement of the learner in Biology. Also ITM was found to be more effective than the conventional method in improving achievement in Biology.

13. Kenneth D. Peterson (1978) investigated into the nature of scientific inquiry instruction for high school students. A model of inquiry was constructed and translated into two instructional programmes for this purpose. The programme was compared with

instruction from a common physics curriculum. Specifically, experimental comparisons were made between (1) General science instruction and narrow focussed inquiry training. (2) Concrete materials based instruction and meaningful verbal learning as per Ausubel.

The dependent variables of the study were 15 scoring items from performance test, concrete materials, and manipulative assessment instrument. The independent variables were 9-week instructional programmes designed to include characteristics of current broad objective science instruction, specific and focussed scientific training, materials manipulation and meaningful verbal learning.

The study sample consisted of 67 subjects enrolled in physics courses of San Jose, California High School. They were divided into three groups.

Group 1: (PP): They completed Project Physics units Five and Six. This instruction consisted of readings, lectures, guided laboratories and pencil paper exams. In addition they designed and built solar hot dog cookers.

Group 2: Completed the same content, with less laboratory time. In addition they received a verbal learning unit (demonstration, lectures, discussing, pencil and paper exams) in scientific inquiry in which observational strategies, questioning, experimental design and reporting were emphasized.

Group 3 (SI): Completed a training programme in scientific inquiry that consisted of eight activity lessons requiring 45 hours. Each lesson began with a discrepant event. The demonstrations were followed by time for individual observing, questioning and designing experiments. Open experimentation time for individual inquiry was provided. Generalizing and communication of findings followed it. Lessons concluded with instructor-guided models of scientific inquiry.

The findings and conclusions of the study were

(1) The value of focussed and inquiry training as opposed to general curriculum was more.
(2) The value of concrete experience for some aspects of scientific inquiry instruction was demonstrated, even for older and

science successful students. These findings were contradictory to what the "meaningful verbal theories" of Ausubel predicted.

(3) The findings supported a model of scientific inquiry performance in which the various processes (e.g., observing, questioning, and designing experiments are not equivalent processes).

(4) No gender differences were detected in the training programme

(5) The training programme was effective in improving performance in a variety of skills.

14. Imelda Rodriguez and Lowell J. Bethel (1983) conducted a study to determine the effectiveness of inquiry approach to science and language teaching. The purpose of the study was to develop classification and oral communication skills of bilingual Mexican American third graders. Random samples consisting of 64 subjects was selected for experimental and control groups from a population of 120 bilingual Mexican American third graders.

The Solomon Four-group experimental design was employed. Pre-testing and post-testing was performed by use of the Goldstein-Sheerer Object Sorting Test (GSOST) and the Test of Oral Communication Skills (TOCS). The experimental group participated in a sequential series of science lessons that required manipulation of objects, exploration, and peer interaction and teacher pupil interaction. The children made observations and comparisons of familiar objects and then grouped them on the basis of perceived and inferred attributes. Children worked individually and in small groups. Analysis of variance procedure was used on the post test scores to determine if there was a significant improvement in classification and oral communication skills in the experimental group.

The results on the post test scores indicated a significant improvement at the 0.01 level for the experimental group in both classification and oral communication skills.

It was concluded that participation in the science inquiry lessons facilitated the development of classification and oral communication skills of bilingual children.

15. Eunice Boyd and Kenneth, D. George. (1973) investigated into the effect of science inquiry on the abstract categorization behaviour of deaf children. Students of the Archbishop Ryan

Memorial Institute for the deaf in Philadelphia between ages 10-13 were subjects of the study and were randomly assigned to an experimental and control group. A programme of 30 sessions of science inquiry was developed. A pre-test/post-test control group design was used. Dual form of the Goldstein-Sheerer Object Sorting test was used.

The results indicated that deaf children could benefit from participation in inquiry based science instruction. The question raised regarding the possibility of inquiry without verbal discussion was resolved when it became evident that the children of the study through several modes of expression (sign language, finger spelling, demonstration, facial expression and lip reading) could communicate effectively with each other.

The results proved that conceptual system of categorization could be developed in deaf children through experiential enrichment, exclusive of language development.

16. Gerald, W. conducted a meta analysis to explore two areas of research. Lott (1983) titled Comparison of inductive versus deductive teaching approaches and the use of Advance organizers

The study involved the coding of 128 characteristics for 39 studies that spanned the period from 1957 through 1980. The coding variables included 57 that were concerned with features of the treatment while 12 were concerned with outcome attributes. Aspects such as research methodology sample characteristics and instructional experiences were examined quantitatively in terms of their relationships to the treatment effects through the use of a common metric for all studies. Mean effect sizes were calculated and reported.

The implications of the study were:

1. Inductive and deductive approach provide a framework for conjectures as well as directions for future research.
2. More research concerning the levels of inquiry needs to be conducted. The study found many studies concerned with inquiry but few addressed the level of inquiry involved.
3. The difference between effect of inquiry experience upon comprehension and process skills needs further exploration.

STUDIES RELATED TO PRE-SERVICE TEACHER EDUCATION IN THE MODELS OF TEACHING

A number of teaching strategies/ models of teaching have been developed by scholars. In the previous section studies related to classroom implementation of the model were discussed. There is no doubt that models of teaching are very useful in enhancing the teaching competence of pre service and in service teachers. There is a definite need to equip student teachers with a variety of teaching techniques so that their teaching behaviour in classroom is more effective leading to improvement in pupil learning.

In this section studies relating to pre-service student teachers, their training needs and effects of training strategies have been discussed.

1. Gary, L. Sweitzer and Ronald, D. Anderson (1983) conducted a meta analysis on studies of teacher education having as measured outcomes one or more variables associated with inquiry teaching. Inquiry addresses those teacher behaviours that facilitate student acquisition of concepts and processes through strategies such as problem solving, uses of evidence, logical and analytical reasoning, clarification of values and decision making. Studies that contained sufficient data for the calculation of an effect size were coded for 114 variables. These variables were divided into six major categories. Study information and design characteristics, teacher and teacher trainee characteristics, student characteristics, treatment description, outcome description and effect size calculation. Mean effect sizes broken across selected variables were calculated.

The major conclusions were summarized as follows: A wide variety of teacher education programmes result in changes in science teacher knowledge, classroom behaviour and attitudes. Whether pre service or in service and located on a university campus or in a school setting, there is a wide variety of potentially successful approaches available to put into practices. Not all the approaches were of equal potential, however, a designer of a teacher education programme could carefully examine the alternative means for achieving various objectives of the programme.

2. The objectives of the study undertaken by Passi, B.K. *et al.*, (1985) was to find out the effectiveness of variations in training

strategies for ITM in terms of understanding, competence, reaction and willingness of student teachers. The students were divided into two groups. The sample was forty-two students drawn from sixteen different secondary teacher-training institutions.

E1 – standard model treatment group (SMT).

E2 – The group having variation in peer practice feed back (PPF)

The study employed pre-test and post-test parallel group design. The experimental group E1 employed standard model treatment (SMT). The treatment included discussion of the concerned model, demonstration and PPF. The parallel group E2 employed modification of standard treatment either in theory or demonstration or PPF or coaching.

The tools developed at Indore in 1985 were translated into regional languages and were as follows:

(1) Bruce Joyce Theory check up for ITM
(2) Indore theory checkup for ITM
(3) Reaction scale for ITM
(4) Teaching Analysis guide for ITM.

Some of the major findings related to ITM were:

(1) Student teachers' of the E1 as well as E2 groups understood the theoretical aspects of ITM to the same extent.
(2) Student teachers of E1 and E2 groups attained competence in ITM to the same degree in the beginning of PPF viewing after demonstrations and after having understood the theory.
(3) Student teachers of group E1 attained significantly higher competence at the end of PPF as compared to student teachers of group E2.
(4) Student teachers of both E1 and E2 had equally favourable reactions towards ITM.

3. The study by Bhagaban, Subudhi. (1991) focussed on training through the inquiry training model of teaching, with variations in demonstrations and peer practice feedback in terms of teaching competencies of student teachers. The efficacy of different variations in the training strategy adopted for training through the inquiry training model of teaching in terms of performance on: (a) Theory check-up (TC) (b) Teaching Assessment guide (TAG) (c) Reaction Scale (RS) was studied. In addition, the feasibility of integrating

training through Inquiry Training model of teaching with practice teaching programme and school teaching in terms of student teachers' and pupils reactions.

Two group pre-test and post-test design was used to study the effectiveness of the training strategy in Inquiry Training model of teaching. The training programme consisted of orientation about the theory of the model, followed by explanation and discussion of (i) Lesson plan guide, (ii) Teaching analysis guide, (iii) Lesson planning. After the orientation viewing of demonstrations lessons were arranged. The subjects observed the demonstration using (TAG). Then they prepared lessons using the model in a small group situation of four peers (quadro). This was further divided into two pairs. Twenty-minute lessons were practiced with peer feedback.

The effectiveness of the training strategy was judged against the criterion variables of: (i) Theoretical understanding; (ii) Reaction towards the model to implement it.

The sample was 24 B.Ed. students of Government College of Karnal who were divided into 2 groups matched on academic qualifications and method subjects offered.

Age, sex, socio-economic status and physical environment were controlled. The two teacher educators who gave demonstration lessons had approximately the same academic qualifications and duration of teaching experience. The subject matter covered by the lessons was from B.Ed syllabus on life sciences. Analysis of variance was applied.

The tools used were:

(a) Indore-theory checkup (Indore, 1986); (b) Reaction scale of ITM (by Malhotra and Sansanwal (1986); (c) Teaching Assessment guide (Malhotra and Sansanwal (1986); (d) Lesson plan guide developed by researcher.

The major findings were:

(1) In theory the two groups of student teachers were initially similar in their pre test scores but later on the attainment of the second group (E2) showed more attainment result than that of first group (E1). The difference of mean scores was significant (E2 >E1).

(2) The two groups of student teachers differed significantly in their attainment in peer practice feedback (E2 > E1).

(3) There was a significant difference of mean scores of theory orientation on the reaction of student teachers (E2 > E1).

(4) There was a significant difference of mean scores of demonstration and peer practice feed back on the reaction of the student-teachers between the groups (E1>E2).

(5) There was a significant difference in the skill of teaching competency as measured by TAG (E2 > E1).

(6) There was no significant difference in the mean scores of reactions of the student teachers towards the teaching delivered by the two groups of student teachers (E1 > E2). [(E2 – demonstration followed by feedback (D1 + peer practice + D2 + feedback + D3 + feedback) and (E1 – demonstration and feed back; a time lag exists. D1 + D2 + D3 + peer practice.)]

4. D' Lima and Lobo (1985) conducted a study to find the effect of a training strategy in ITM on Graduate student teachers.

Seventy-two student teachers were exposed to theory cum demonstration sessions on ITM for three days. At the end of the programme they were tested for the theoretical understanding of the model using Bruce Joyce Marsha Weil Theory Check Up (BTC). The mean BTC score was much higher than expected chance score.

To know whether it is necessary to have high reasoning ability for better understanding of the ITM, the student teachers were given Abstract Reasoning Test from the Differential Aptitude Test prepared by Bennett, Seashore and Wesman. There was a significant difference in the mean BTC Scores of High Abstract Reasoning groups compared to their counterparts of Low Abstract Reasoning groups.

They studied the reaction of the student teachers. They grouped them into two groups: (a) Student teachers with High Theoretical Understanding and Low Theoretical Understanding of ITM, (b) Student teachers with High Abstract Reasoning (HAR) and Low Abstract Reasoning (LAR). Reactions were measured by using the scale developed by Passi and Sansanwal (1985).

The results showed that the group with High Theoretical Understanding did not find it difficult to understand the puzzling problem. The groups High on Theoretical Understanding and High on Abstract Reasoning felt that the model is conducive to develop scientific process skills.

5. D'Lima and Sugandhi (1986) have tried to find out the intellectual and emotional responses of the trainees towards ITM.

Seventy-six graduate student teachers were trained in ITM through theory lectures and demonstrations. To test their theoretical understanding the Bruce Joyce and Marsha Weil Theory Checkup (BTC) was administered. The mean BTC score was less than that of D'Lima and Lobo (1985) study, yet it was still higher than the expected chance score which the subject could earn without knowing anything about the model.

To find out if there was any significant difference on theoretical understanding between the group High on Abstract Reasoning and the group Low on Abstract Reasoning the t-test analysis was done. The study did not indicate any significant difference in the mean BTC scores (t value was insignificant). Thus abstract reasoning ability did not influence the theoretical understanding of ITM in this study.

The researcher prepared a reaction scale consisting of 23 items. Item analysis was undertaken. The group Low on Abstract Reasoning felt that it was difficult to analyze the thinking process of pupils while teaching through this model. The group high on theoretical understanding and the group high on abstract reasoning was of the opinion that teaching through this model make the pupils alert and attentive during the lesson. The groups low on theoretical understanding and low on abstract reasoning felt that they were not competent to handle various phases of the model. The group low on theoretical understanding felt that strict adherence to the rules of the model destroyed the pupils creative spirit. The group low on abstract reasoning was of the opinion that teaching through this model is time consuming and yet there is no thorough understanding of the subject matter. The group high on theoretical understanding was of the opinion that the model trains the pupils to differ judgement. The group high on abstract reasoning was of the opinion that the model teaches the pupils to ask pin-pointed questions. The group high on theoretical understanding was of the opinion that the model requires insightful teachers.

6. D'Lima and Sugandhi (1986) developed a willingness questionnaire and administered it to the student teachers after training them in ITM. The results showed that graduate student teachers trained in ITM were willing to use the model even if it was not made compulsory. They also showed a desire to undergo further training in the model and act as resource persons. Majority of students were ready to implement ITM in schools.

7. Pandey, A. (1981) evolved teaching styles on the basis of verbal interaction taking place in the classroom; determined the effect of teaching style on science concept attainment at various levels.

The sample comprised 24 postgraduates, trained male science teachers having at least five years of teaching experience in secondary and higher secondary schools and 300 secondary school students studying in class XI of five schools of Varanasi. Concept attainment test and Instrument for Analysing Verbal teaching behaviour developed by investigator, Group Test of general mental ability (Joshi), calculation of percentages, different interaction analysis ratios, analysis of variance and t-test were used. He found that all behaviours were not frequently observed in the science teachers. Extended lecturing was negatively related with different levels of concept attainment and the segment of formal level, excepting for segment of problems and definitions with which it was positively correlated. The teachers questioning had a significant positive effect on both the levels, classificatory and formal of concept attainment. Teaching styles had varying effects on both the levels of concept attainment as well as total concept attainment. Empathic and democratic teaching styles were on par as regards their effect on concept attainment even though the empathic style was slightly superior to the democratic style. Oratorical and traditional styles were inferior to empathic and democratic teaching styles. Giving background information, encouraging students participation and students responses and giving ample opportunity for students to think in the course of teaching behaviours were conducive to better concept learning.

8. Kamlesh, Chaudary (1986) conducted a study to identify skills needed to implement CAM and ITM. He used a skill-based approach to train pre service teachers in models of teaching—CAM and ITM. He trained the student teachers to teach concepts through CAM and problem/principles through ITM and facts through

modified Herbartian steps. Thus both conventional and skill based training approaches were used.

The conclusions drawn from the study are

(1) It is feasible to train pre service teachers in the skill of fluency in questioning and citing examples through micro teaching and CAM resulting in increase in skill competency.
(2) It is feasible to train pre service teachers in the skills of problem solving through micro teaching and ITM resulting in increase in skill competency.
(3) It is feasible to train pre service teachers in ITM using skill-based approach.
(4) Pre service teachers trained in CAM and ITM are able to incorporate the model in their school-based practice teaching resulting in improvement in student's achievement and teaching competencies of teachers.

9. Ajit Singh (1990) undertook a study to determine the relative effectiveness of three training strategies in the training of student teachers in the Advance Organizer Model of Teaching. In the first phase teacher educators were trained in the models of teaching. At the end of their training it was ensured that they had developed an adequate understanding of the Advance Organizer Model (AOM).

The three training strategies were

(1) SMT: Presentation of theory, followed by whole demonstration and discussion.
(2) MMT 1: Presentation of theory, followed by phase wise demonstration and discussion.
(3) MMT 2: Presentation of Demonstration, followed by presentation of theory, followed by phase wise demonstration and discussion.

The sample of the study consisted of 252 - secondary student teachers belonging to ten secondary colleges of education in the country. The students belonged to different subject areas and had different educational qualifications.

The tools used were:

1. Theory check up scale developed by Sansanwal and Buddhisagar.
2. Teaching Analysis Guide (TAG)

3. General Reaction Scale
4. Specific Instructional Effects Scale.

The major findings of the study were

1. The training strategy MMT2 was found to be more effective than other strategies SMT and MMT1, in terms of developing theoretical understanding of AOM.
2. The training strategy MMT1 was found to be more effective than SMT and MMT2 strategies in terms of developing competence in AOM and SMT was more effective than MMT2. When the groups were matched with respect to abstract reasoning, MMT1, strategy was found to be significantly more effective than SMT and MMT2.
3. All the student teachers in different groups trained through different training strategies developed favourable reactions towards AOM. All strategies were found to be equally effective in terms of reactions towards the model.
4. The AOM was found to be an effective instructional effect—Talking with others in an organized way, applying knowledge creatively, understanding what is said to him, first stating important points and then giving details and presenting data meaningfully.

10.The study by Buddhisagar, M. (1990) examined the achievement of students through the developed instructional material in relation to the learner's characteristics such as intelligence, creativity, attitude towards teaching profession, and personality.

The study was carried out in two stages. At the first stage instructional materials were developed. For this 109 B.Ed students admitted during the 1983-84 academic session to the University teaching Department of Education, Indore were taken. The students were at least second class graduates in Arts and Science.

In the second stage 139 students admitted during 1985-86 session were taken. These students were divided into three groups of 39, 55 and 45 students. All male students were clubbed in III group. In each group there were graduates and post-graduates from science and arts faculties.

The study was based on control group design. There were three levels of treatment and three groups of students. The treatments were randomly assigned to the three groups. Group I received treatment of linear programmed material, Group II received treatment of Advanced Organizer material, Group III was given treatment of traditional material and Group IV was called as control group. Topics were from Educational Psychology Course of B.Ed students. Each unit was to be completed in one week. At the end of each unit an achievement test was administered to all the three groups. The achievement of the students on the criterion tests and their reactions towards the instructional material constituted the dependent variables. The attitudes towards teaching profession, creativity, extraversion-introversion were the moderate variables. Intelligence was controlled through statistical manipulation by using Analysis of Co-variance Techniques.

Tools used for Data collection were

1. Raven's Advance Progressive Matrices (1971).
2. Attitude scale developed by Katti and Bannur (1974).
3. Creativity was measured by using Torrance Test of Creative Thinking.
4. The Extroversion-Introversion trait of personality was measured with the help of Maudsley-Personality Inventory.
5. Achievement was measured with the help of the test developed by the investigator.
6. Reaction scales to know the reaction of the student's towards the instructional materials were developed by investigator

The major findings reported were

1. The overall mean achievement scores of the students taught by Advanced Organizer Model was better than that of the operant conditioning model. But both experimental groups were superior to control group.
2. Intelligent student's achievement was high in all the three groups.
3. Attitude towards teaching profession did not significantly affect overall achievement.
4. Personality and creativity did not effect achievement.
5. It was found out that low intelligence students could be taught effectively using Advance Organizer Model whereas high intelligence students could be taught by either of the two models.

6. There was no significant effect of the interaction between (a) Intelligence and creativity (b) Treatment and personality (c) Treatment and creativity (d) Treatment and attitude (e) creativity and personality (f) attitude and Intelligence, personality and creativity on over all achievement.
7. Students belonging to different levels of intelligence, creativity, extroversion-introversion dimensions of personality and attitude towards the teaching profession had equally favourable reactions towards the instructional material based on the Advance Organizer Model and based on Operant Conditioning Model.

11. The study by Bhoodev Singh (1986) was designed to find out the effect of micro teaching based practice teaching, using skill training with micro teaching, and teaching models based practice teaching on teaching of prospective teachers. The experimental design was pretest-post test design. The sample consisted of 30 prospective teachers. They were selected randomly from Sultanpur district. The sample was divided into three groups:

Group A: For conventional programme of practice teaching without using micro teaching.

Group B: For practice teaching using micro teaching

Group C: For practice teaching using skill training with micro teaching and teaching models based training.

The tools used for collection of data were

1. Teaching competence assessment scale developed by Jangira, Singh and Sabharwal.
2. Teacher attitude inventory by Ahluwalia. Skills used in the study were: (a) Reinforcement (b) Questioning (c) Illustrating with examples. (d) Explaining (e) Stimulus variation and (f) Class room management.

Data was analysed using Analysis of Covariance. The results of the study were: Micro teaching based practice teaching and model based practice teaching were found to be significantly more effective to develop teaching competence among prospective teachers than the conventional programme of practice teaching.

The effect of micro teaching or skill based practice teaching was not significant to develop prospective teachers attitude towards teaching in the short duration of the experiment.

12. In a study by Das, B.C. (1993) an attempt was made to ascertain specifically whether teaching through a particular model, i.e., CAM would emerge as an effective strategy of training which would be acceptable to a teacher educator for providing training to new entrants. The effectiveness has been tested in terms of teaching competence among the student teachers.

The sample consisted of 16 students studying in B.Ed B section (1989-90) of Univ. Dept. of Education, Indore. A pre-test/post-test one group experiment design was adopted.

In order to collect relevant data the following tools were used:

(a) Theory check up Test (Bruce Joyce-1978)
(b) Modified theory check up (Sansanwal-1985)
(c) Reaction scale (Passi and Sansanwal)
(d) Teaching analysis guide (Bruce Joyce)

The effectiveness of training in CAM was studied in terms of theoretical understanding of the model, its practice, coaching in school, reaction of student teachers and their previous academic achievement related means, Coefficient of variation, Rank order correlation and t test were statistical tools used.

Findings and Implication reported are

1. Concept attainment model is effective in developing the teaching competencies of pre service teachers.
2. Training given to student teachers increases understanding about the theoretical aspects of CAM.
3. Training in CAM has effected teaching behaviour of student teachers and hence CAM is effective in terms of training.
4. CAM effected the teaching behaviour of student teachers at coaching stage.
5. The training process from theory to practice has brought about significant changes in student teachers reaction towards CAM.
6. There is no significant relationship between previous academic achievement of student teachers and their performance on CAM at theory and coaching stages.

13. Kamlesh, Chaudary (1989) undertook an experiment to find out if student teachers trained to teach concepts in science through CAM would indirectly learn the teaching skills without any formal training and be equally competent in using those skills for teaching facts, problems, etc., through traditional training.

Ten students trained in CAM participated in the experiment I. After completion of the experiment I, student teachers were given orientation in planning lessons, according to traditional teaching based on Herbartian steps. They were then exposed to demonstration lessons in Physics, Chemistry and Biology. Each student was then given one unit to be taught in schools. The content analysis of the units was done and they taught concepts through CAM and facts through traditional teaching. Two lessons in CAM and two lessons in TT of each student were rated by the investigator on Process Appraisal Scale of Teacher Effectiveness (PASTE).

Major conclusions drawn from the study were:

Student teacher performed equally competently while teaching through both the methods even though no specific training was given during the college based training either in various skills or in traditional teaching.

It was found that skills learnt in CAM were easily transferred to traditional teaching. In some cases, especially for the skills of evaluation and explaining since more scope is available in traditional teaching for exhibition of these skills, there was a marked improvement in performance. Skills of set induction and set closure were also learnt indirectly through practice in traditional teaching since they cannot be used in CAM.

14.Richard, L. Campbell (1979) tried to investigate the relationship between Reading comprehension of pre service and in service elementary teachers and process skill instruction.

The process skills are methods of investigation used for solving problems. The researcher has identified two kinds of process skills taught in science. They are:

(i) Basic process skills that include measuring, observing, classifying, communicating, inferring, using space time relations and predicting.

(ii) Integrated process skills that are more complex are designed to promote the retention and refinement of basic process skills. They are identifying variables, formulating hypothesis, interpreting data, controlling variables, operationally defining variables, and designing investigations.

The subjects (n=44) for this investigation were in two intact groups. One group consisting of Junior and seniors (n=27) and the other graduate students (n=17) enrolled in a competency based science methods course.

The students worked on the Basic Science Process Skills (BSPS) programme and Integrated Science Process Skills (ISPS) programmes. The total time the two groups spent on each programme was the same. The tools used were BSPSAT, ISPSAT and Nelson-Denny comprehension reading test.

The main findings reported are

(1) Pre service and In service teacher reading comprehension can be significantly improved with process skill instruction. According to Suchman (1960) and Ervin (1960) one of the advantages in teaching science process skills is its transfer effect to other academic disciplines.
(2) The data collected revealed no significant difference between in service and pre service teachers reading comprehension scores.
(3) The link between integrated process skills and reading comprehension was stronger than the link between basic process skills and reading comprehension in this study.
(4) The study implies the need for reading experts to examine closely the inclusion of science process skills in reading models.

15. Lazarowitz, R. and Lee (1976) undertook a study to develop an instrument to determine the inquiry attitudes of secondary science teachers.

Eighty-three items of inquiry were identified by the researchers to form the first instrument based on the following sources: Bruner (1961), Lee (1960), McRel BSCS (1969), NSTA (1971), Schwab (1963), and Steiner (1970).

The items selected referred to three areas: classroom teacher-student interaction, laboratory investigations and textbooks used.

Half the statements were positively formulated towards inquiry strategy and half negatively. The instrument, Inquiry Science Teaching Strategies (ISTS) used a five point scale in which a subject responded Strongly Agree (SA), Agree (A), Neutral (N), Disagree (D), Strongly Disagree (SD).

The instrument was submitted to seven professors of science education (a panel of judges) who were asked to evaluate each item on the basis of whether or not it represented inquiry strategy. With some slight rewording items receiving a majority of votes (7-0, 6-1, 5-2) were considered for selection on the final instrument.

Thirty secondary science teacher responses to the ISTS provided data for Item analysis. Programme TESTAT (Veldman, 1967) computed a biserial correlation coefficient for each item was similar to the result obtained with the group of 30 teachers. Forty items, which correlated higher than 0.25 with the total score and which were recommended by the panel of judges, were selected for the final instrument.

Construct validity was achieved by the technique of known groups (Shaw & Wright, 1967). The final 40 item instrument was administered to 4 other groups in addition to Group 1 (seven judges).

Group 1: It included science educators.

Group 2: It included graduate students in doctoral programmes who were trained in inquiry approach.

Group 3: It included in service secondary science teachers who were trained in inquiry approach in a 4-day workshop.

Group 4: It included student teacher in their first day of class in the methods course.

Group 5: It included secondary science teachers without training in inquiry approach.

Construct validity was achieved by obtaining the group mean score of the attitude scale. Alpha coefficient of internal consistency was computed. An F test was computed for determining the overall differences among the five groups mean scores on ISTS.

The results of the study suggested that ISTS could be employed to determine the inquiry attitudes of secondary science teachers. ISTS also makes it possible to make a comparison of the degree of acceptance of the inquiry approach by different groups.

16. Lazarowitz, R, *et al.*, (1978) investigated into the relationship between student teachers characteristics and their attitudes towards inquiry. In this study two demographic variables gender and age and five background variables desire to teach, GPA, academic status, semester hours in education courses were selected to be investigated.

Two samples participated in the study:

Group A: Forty-four secondary science student teachers: (Twenty-five females and nineteen males, fall 1973). Their range in science courses was 0-70 hr and in educational courses was 0-35 hr.

Group B: Ninety-eight elementary science education majors (all females, spring 1974). Their GPA range was from 2.0 to 4.0. The sample consisted of forty-six juniors, forty-five senior and seven graduate students. Their age range was nineteen-twenty-seven years old. Their range in science courses was 0-35 hr and in educational courses 0-75hrs.

The study followed a one group pretest-post test design. Inquiry science teaching strategies (ISTS) instrument (Lazarowitz and Lee, 1976) in a modified form was used for obtaining a score for each subject as an indication of his attitude towards inquiry.

The findings showed that at the end of the methods courses both the Group A and B showed positive attitudes towards inquiry. The Group A, which had more semester hours in science courses, held more favourable attitudes towards the inquiry approach. Semester hours in educational courses and gender did not effect attitude scores. In the Group B, higher desire to teach, higher GPA, high academic status, older in age, more semester hours in education courses had a positive effect on the favourable attitudes towards inquiry strategies. But number of semester hours in science courses was not significant in determining more favourable attitude towards inquiry.

17. Bihari (1986) studied the effectiveness of three training strategies in learning CAM in terms of understanding of the model; in terms of teaching competency of student teachers; in terms of: (a) coaching through the model (b) reaction towards the model and (c) willingness to implement the model.

The sample consisted of 55 student teachers studying in B.Ed 'B' section of the Department of Education, D.A.V. Indore. Theory check up by Bruce Joyce and modified theory check up (Indore), Teaching Analysis Guide (TAG), Reaction Scale, Willingness Scale, ANOVA, ANCOVA and 't' test were utilized. The researcher found that the three training strategies, namely, peer feed back and practice in pairs and demonstration followed by practice in quadro peer feed back and practice in pairs and demonstration followed by practice in quadro were equally effective for developing teaching competence.

18. Antimdas (1986) developed the model competency of pre-service teacher trainees by adopting CAM with three different training strategies. He studied the effectiveness of the training strategy in terms of model competency acquired by the pre-service teacher trainees at the end of the coaching stage. He also studied the effect of personality factors A, B, C, E, F, G, H, I, L, M, N, O, Q1, Q2, Q3 and Q4 separately on the model competency acquired by three training strategies in CAM at the end of training stage. The effect of personality factors and the interaction between personality factors was separately studied at the end of coaching stage.

The sample consisted of fifty-five B.Ed. students of Education Department of DAV, Indore, 16 P.F. Cattell, Teaching Analysis guide by Bruce Joyce, Factorial Analysis of Variance with unequal cell size and one way Analysis of Variance was utilised.

He found that three different training strategies were equally effective in terms of model competency of teacher trainees at the end of training and coaching stage. The personality factors did not influence the model competency of teacher trainees at the end of coaching stage. The personality factors influenced significantly the competency of teacher trainees at the end of coaching stage. There was no significant effect of interaction between treatment and personality factors separately on model competency of teacher trainees at the end of training and coaching stage.

STUDIES RELATED TO TEACHER EDUCATORS' ATTITUDES TOWARDS INNOVATIONS/MODELS OF TEACHING

1. Passi, B.K., Singh, L.C., and Sansanwal, D.N. (1989) undertook a study to develop an effective strategy of training in models of teaching. The effectiveness of training was judged against the criteria of theoretical understanding of and reaction towards the structure and functions of models. Better understanding coupled with favourable attitudes is likely to result in acceptability and willingness for implementation. Therefore the training effectiveness was judged in terms of willingness to implement the models of teaching in teacher training programmes.

A single group pre test and post test design was used to study the effectiveness of training strategy in case of the two models of teaching, i.e., Concept Attainment Model (CAM) and Inquiry Training Model (ITM). The training programme consisted of orientation about the theory of the model followed by explanation and discussion of (i) Lesson plan guide (LPG); (ii) Teaching Analysis Guide (TAG) and (iii) Lesson Planning (LP). After the orientation, viewing of the demonstration lesson was arranged. The subjects observed the demonstration lesson using TAG. The subjects then prepared lessons using the models in a small group situation of quadros. They were further divided into two pairs. When one student teacher was teaching in a quadro situation his pair partner was observing him on TAG for giving feed back at the end of the lesson. Pair partner who was observed by the other pair partner gave the next lesson on model. Thus twenty-minute lessons were practiced and five-minute feed back was given. This procedure was used for both CAM and ITM.

The programme was of fifty- six-hour duration. A purposive sample of forty- five teacher educators was taken. They represented twenty-five institutions from nine states and two union territories.

Measurement tools used were

1. Theory check-up for CAM (Bruce Joyce)
2. Indore theory check-up for CAM
3. Reaction scale on CAM
4. Theory check-up for ITM (Bruce Joyce)
5. Indore Theory Check-up for ITM
6. Reaction scale on ITM

7. Willingness scale for implementation of the models.

The major findings were

i. Training in CAM in the form of lecture demonstration, discussion and peer practice and feed back did enhance the teacher educators understanding of theoretical aspects of CAM. Training did bring out significant favourable change in the teacher educators' reactions towards CAM. Level of understanding of CAM did not influence the teacher educator's reactions towards CAM.

ii. Training in ITM did influence the understanding of theoretical concepts of ITM. Training did bring about favourable reactions towards ITM. Level of understanding of ITM did not influence the teacher educator's reactions towards ITM.

iii. The teacher educators were willing to implement the models of teaching in teacher education programmes if some support system was available.

2. The study undertaken by Valand, J.B. (1983) was to develop an instrument seeking to identify and quantify four aspects of innovative proneness of teacher educators. They are: (i) teacher educators general attitudes towards change or change related values (ii) teacher educators preferred behaviours in reaction to their perception of the attitudes to innovations (iii) teacher educators attitudes towards specific innovations (iv) teacher educators preferred behaviours in relation to innovation implementation.

An innovative proneness scale was constructed and standardized and was used for studying innovative proneness of 200 primary teacher educators of Gujarat. There were three sections:

(i) Attitude to innovation scale
(ii) Situational and innovation characteristics
(iii) Change related values questionnaire.

Percentile norms were established. 't' test was used to test the significance of difference between means of two groups with age, sex, experience, qualification as variables.

Major findings reported were

(1) The mean innovative proneness score of teachers above 35 years of age was greater than those teachers whose age is less than 35 years.

(2) The mean scores of female teachers were higher than that of male teachers.

(3) The mean score of teachers having more than five years of teaching experience was greater.

(4) Teachers having a M.A. degree had the highest mean score while those with B.Sc. degree had the lowest score on the innovative proneness scale.

(5) The mean score of teachers who had attended in service programmes was higher than those who had not attended any in service programme.

(6) The components of the innovative proneness scale significantly correlated with teachers personal variable such as age, sex, experience, academic qualifications, professional qualifications and in service education.

3. The major objectives of the study by Gulati, K.C. (1980) was to find out how the different subgroups of teachers classified according to certain personal characteristics differed in their predisposition to adjust to innovations.

The sample consisted of 372 teachers drawn from thirty-eight higher secondary schools in Union territory of Delhi. Data was collected using educational innovation attitude scale. 't' test, product moment correlation and stepwise regression analysis was used.

The major findings were

There was no significant difference between the mean predisposition scores of the male and female teachers; younger and older teachers; those having five years and more than five years teaching experience; and those having bachelor's or master's degree. Teachers who were professionally satisfied were significantly better predisposed to adopt innovations than those who were professionally not satisfied.

4. The main objectives of the study conducted by B.R. Panchal (1977) was to construct and study the innovative proneness scale for teacher educators of secondary teachers training colleges of Gujarat with respect of age, experience, sex, professional satisfaction, mobility, participation in in-service education, habit of reading professional literature, professional training and academic qualifications.

The sample of the study included 200 teacher educators of all the secondary teacher training colleges of Gujarat State. The innovative proneness scale was developed and used to collect data from the teacher educators. Percentile ranks, 't' test and factor analysis was used to analyze the data.

The major findings were

(i) Teacher educators above thirty-five years of age were more change prone than those below thirty-five years.

(ii) Teacher educators with more experience perceived the importance of teaching resources in a better way.

(iii) Academic qualifications of the teacher educators bore no significant relationship with attitudes to innovation on the whole. But teacher educators with master's degree showed significantly higher change proneness.

(iv) Professional qualifications did not have significant relationship with teacher educator's attitude to innovation, but those with M.Ed. degree showed significant concern for teaching learning process.

(v) Mobile teacher educators were more venturesome and more prone to change.

(vi) In service education of teacher educators tended to be significantly related to attitudes to innovation, teaching resources, concern with teaching learning process and school community relationship.

CONCLUSION

An overview of the related studies reveals that there is awareness among educators to adopt inquiry method of teaching in order to increase students active participation in the class room situation, to promote their creative thinking and as a result to enable them to master the content very effectively. Some studies have shown that inquiry method is superior to traditional method in helping students to develop most of the instructional outcomes. A number of studies have recommended the use of inquiry mode of instruction. Inquiry approach has been found to be more effective in comparison to traditional approach in improving students questioning ability, their science process skills, their verbal creativity and achievement.

The studies on training pre service teacher educators in the use of models have shown that student teachers are receptive to models. Student teachers are found to be having positive attitudes towards models of teaching and were willing to implement the models. Different training strategies adopted were found to be effective in increasing student teachers competence.

Most of the studies on pre service teacher education were based on providing training in models of teaching using micro teaching approach. Generally a pre-test/post-test single group or parallel group design was adopted. Passi, *et al.*, have tried to find out the theoretical understanding, attitudes and willingness of student teachers using a pre-test/post-test parallel group design. Training consisted of theoretical orientation, demonstration and practice with peer group feedback in pairs or quadros.

D'Lima, *et al.*, conducted studies to test the teaching competence of student teachers after giving them training in ITM using micro-teaching approach. One group pre-test/post-test design was used.

Ajit Singh studied the relative effectiveness of three training strategies in Advance Organizer Model. He used a single group post-test design in which, only post-test training effects were studied. The training strategies were variations in theory presentation, demonstration and discussion.

Bihari also studied the post-test effects of training strategies, which had variations in feedback procedures. He used ANOVA and ANCOVA techniques to study the relative effectiveness of the training strategies.

These studies were mainly helpful in developing the method and procedure adopted in the present study. A notable feature is that in the extensive literature reviewed in the present study, there has been no recorded evidence of any research work having been carried out on models of teaching in the state of Andhra Pradesh, India along the lines identified in the foregoing conclusion.

It is in this context that the present study becomes important and essential as endorsed by the specific concerns of earlier researchers both in aims of the study and its procedures.

Research Methodology

INTRODUCTION

The previous three chapters were devoted to presenting the significance of the problem under investigation and for reviewing related literature. In this chapter, the procedure of the research study undertaken is described in detail. The major research question is related to the training needs of the student teachers in models of teaching and innovative readiness of teacher educators.

The objectives of the study are centred on the teacher educators and student teachers. One objective is to find out the willingness of teacher educators to implement models of teaching. In other words, it helps to determine if teacher educators are prepared to teach student teachers, the models of teaching. The second objective is related to the innovative readiness of the student teachers and their training needs. The third objective was to design training strategies with variations in sample size and training techniques. The effectiveness of training strategies is to be determined in terms of theoretical competence, attitude development, and willingness to implement models of teaching.

Any research study involves the elements of observation, description, and analysis of what happens under certain circumstances. Best and Kahn (1989) have evolved a simple three-point analysis to classify educational research. It is as follows:

1. **Historical Research**: It describes 'What was?' The process involves investigating, recording, analysing, and interpreting the events of the past for the purpose of discovering relationships. The generalizations are helpful in understanding the past and the present, and to a very limited extent, in anticipating the future.
2. **Descriptive Research:** It describes 'What is?' The process involves describing, recording, analysing, and interpreting conditions that exist. It involves some type of comparison or contrast and attempts to discover relationships between existing non-manipulated variables.
3. **Experimental Research**: It describes 'What will be?' The process involves deliberate manipulation of certain variables with certain others being suppressed. The focus is on establishment of variable relationships.

The present study comprises both descriptive and experimental types of research. It is descriptive because an attempt was made to find out the willingness of teacher educators to implement models of teaching using a normative survey willingness scale.

The investigator assumed that teacher educators have knowledge of and orientation towards models of teaching. No attempt was made to provide training to teacher educators. Their opinions were gathered by administering the willingness scale.

The study is experimental to the extent that an attempt was made to manipulate the responses of student teachers by providing training. Variations in training schedules were developed. An attempt was made to establish a logical association between training strategies and observed respondent effects.

The design of the study is diagrammatically represented in Fig. 4.1:

Fig. 4.1

RESEARCH DESIGN

No.	*Objective*	*Source and Method of Data Gathering*	*Sampling and Sample Size*	*Tools*	*Method of Analysis*
1.	Willingness of Teacher Educators to implement Models of teaching	Teacher Educators of Nagarjuna University. Administration of Willingness scale	Incidental Sampling n=51	Willingness Scale	Chi-Square Test
2. & 3.	Study of relative effectiveness of training strategies	Student teachers of teacher education colleges of Nagarjuna University. Simple Experiments Design	Random Sampling n=233	Theory Checkup Reaction and Willingness Scale	Anova with 'F' test

SAMPLING PROCEDURES

Fifty-one teacher educators representing different teaching faculties of the nine teacher education colleges of Nagarjuna University out of total population of eighty were chosen. The sampling procedure adopted was incidental sampling. All teacher educators who are accessible were administered the willingness scale.

TEACHER EDUCATORS

The variables chosen for teacher educators' samples were sex, educational qualifications, courses handled experience as teacher educators, and in service education received.

(i) Sex

The population of teacher educators has more number of women teacher educators than men. It is a general opinion that women teacher educators are conservative and traditional compared to men. If that is the case then men should be more willing to be innovative than women should.

(ii) Educational Qualifications

The minimum qualification required to be a teacher educator is two post graduate degrees, viz., one in the basic discipline and other in education. Very few of the teacher educators find time to go in for higher academic qualifications in education like M.Phil. and Ph.D. The research exposure is thus generally limited to the dissertation submitted at the Master of Education level. Hence, it is expected that innovative readiness and research aptitude of the group with research degree is more than those with minimum prescribed qualification.

(iii) Courses Handled

The curriculum for student teachers at Bachelor of Education degree level consists of six courses. Out of them two are methods of teaching school subjects. The teacher educators who handle methods courses generally handle a foundation course also. There are some teachers educators who handle foundation courses only. It is the 'methods' teacher educators who are more likely to implement innovations like micro teaching, team teaching, etc. There is likelihood that 'methods' course teacher educators are more innovative and willing to try out new techniques of teacher education.

(iv) Teaching Experience as Teacher Educator

It is generally believed that older you grow, the more traditional you become. It is believed that those who are in the beginning stages of their teaching experience are young and energetic and more likely to change their techniques. It may be likely that those with less experience may be more innovative and prone to experimentation in the field of teaching than those with more than ten years of teaching experience.

(v) Attendance at In Service Programmes

In the field of teacher education, a number of in service programmes are organized for teacher educators. Participation in-service programmes helps in updating one's knowledge. It is probably that the participants are exposed to the latest techniques, innovations, and changes. It is thus expected that those who attend in service programmes tend to show more innovativeness than those who don't attend do.

Figure 4.2 shows the sample description of teacher educators with regard to the five variables chosen for the present study.

Fig. 4.2

SAMPLE DESCRIPTION OF TEACHER EDUCATORS

S.No	*Variable*		*Sample Size*
1.	Sex	Men	29
		Women	22
2.	Educational Qualifications	Only PG.	35
		M. Phil./Ph.D	16
3.	Courses Handled	Foundation Courses only	10
		Methods Courses	41
4.	Teaching Experience as Teacher Educator	> 10 Years	37
		< 10 Years	14
5.	Attendance at in service Programmes	Yes	34
		No	17

STUDENT TEACHERS

Two hundred and thirty-three student teachers representing four out of the nine colleges of Education of Nagarjuna University were chosen to conduct the 'Simple Experiments Design' study. The four colleges were chosen by a draw of lots. The groups were assigned to different treatments by simple random technique of draw of lots. Thus, to conduct the 'Simple Experiments Design' which is a randomized group design, random allotment of student groups to treatment was adopted.

The total number of student teachers enrolled under the Nagarjuna University area colleges are about 1,600. Out of them, about four hundred and eighty opt for physical science teaching as one of their methods course. The present study had two hundred thirty-three as sample size that is nearly fifty per cent of the population.

The sample comprises forty per cent boys and sixty per cent girl students. It has equal percentage of those with high academic achievement at Graduation level (i.e., 60 % and above) and lower achievement (i.e., 40 - 50 %).

Thus the sample chosen is homogenous and contains students of all categories, and hence representative.

EXPERIMENTAL DESIGN

The student-teacher data was gathered by using 'Simple Methods Experiment' design. It is pictorially represented in Fig. 4.3.

Fig. 4.3

Pictorial Representation of Experimental Design

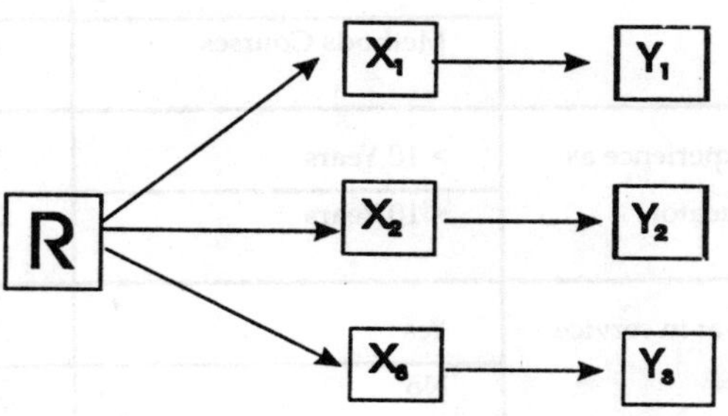

Where: R — — represents Randomized Group Selection
X_1, X_2, X_3, — — represents various Treatment Groups.
Y_1, Y_2, Y_3, — — — represents the post-test effect measurement

Lewis (1968) has explicitly described this method as 'Simple Methods Experiment' design. Kerlinger (1964) has also described this method as One Way Analysis of Variance design.

The investigator used this design to study the relative effectiveness of six training strategies. The six strategies were divided into two groups based on sample size. They are:

(i) Small group approaches (n = 15 to 20)
(ii) Large group approaches (n = 50 to 75)

There were three strategies each in the large groups and small groups based on the type of treatment given. The six strategies were named as follows:

Small Group Approaches

Group A: Only Instructional Material group.
Group B: Conventional Teaching group.
Group C: Training Module Approach group.

Large Group Approaches

Group D: Only Instructional Material group.
Group E: Conventional Teaching group.
Group F: Training Module Approach group.

Instructional Material Groups (Groups A & D)

The investigator prepared a detailed handout about models of teaching. It contains a description of various phases of models. In particular ITM has been described (Appendix A). A lesson plan has been included (Appendix B). The lesson is a physical science lesson on 'Black bodies'. Groups A and D were thus exposed to theoretical background of ITM only. It was attempted to find out whether mere theoretical exposure could develop required attitudes and willingness also in addition to the theoretical understanding gained.

Conventional Teaching Groups (Groups B & E)

The general technique of teaching any 'method' in the science methods course is lecture demonstration followed by discussion. The demonstration here has a slightly different connotation. The teacher educator first gives a descriptive lecture about models of teaching and ITM, the rules to be followed and the salient features.

Then the demonstration is with the student teachers themselves acting as subjects. They are presented with a discrepant event.

They gather data using principles of ITM. They follow the steps of ITM and arrive at a possible explanation. Thus they are practically exposed to the model in action and hence get a clear insight into the working of the model.

Finally a discussion is carried out in the form of question-answer sessions to identify unclear concepts and to clear doubts.

Group B and Group E were exposed to such a treatment. They were not supplied with the handouts but the teacher educator used the same example as given in the handout.

Training Module Approach Group (Groups C & F)

The groups (C and F) were first given the handouts. They thus had a prior knowledge of the model. They were then exposed to a lecture-demonstration session as explained above. The whole group was divided into sub-groups of five to ten students. They had group work and prepared a lesson plan of ITM. This activity was followed by group discussion. Each group presented its lesson and the other groups reacted to it.

EXPERIMENTAL VALIDITY

An experiment can yield honest results only if the design is valid. There are two types of experimental validity – Internal Validity and External Validity.

Internal Validity

An experiment has internal validity if the independent variable produces a genuine effect on the dependent variable in the experimental setting. The external validity on an experiment is the extent to which the variable relationship can be generalized to other settings. Experimental validity is ideal to aspire for because it is likely that it cannot be completely achieved. Too much experimental control to achieve internal validity may reduce external validity. So, some compromise between internal and external validity is inevitable (Best and Kahn, 1989).

Threats to Internal Validity

In educational experiments, a number of extraneous variables are present in the situation. Sometimes they are generated by the experimental design and procedures followed. These variables may influence the results of the experiment.

Before claiming that the selected independent variable has effected the dependent variable, it must be ascertained that the following variables didn't produce the effect and can be mistaken to be the effect of independent variable.

In the present investigation, it was attempted to minimize the threat to internal validity caused by the variables in the manner described.

(i) History, Maturation and Mortality

The short duration of the training schedule (two to four hours) and period of the total experiment (two weeks) help to ensure that the change in subjects was due to training and not due to maturation. No specific incident was noticed during the training period that could have influenced the student teachers. No student dropped out of the schedule. Hence the effect due to above mentioned three influences was minimized to a large extent.

(ii) Pre-testing

Pre-testing may produce practice effect on student teachers resulting in their proficient performance on post-test. This was avoided by using post-test comparisons only.

(iii) Instrumentation

The willingness scales and reaction scale used were adapted versions of standardized tools. Experts validated the final tools used in the investigation and reliability was found to be in the accepted range. Experts also validated the theory check up prepared by investigator and its reliability was estimated to be in the accepted range.

(iv) Statistical Regression

The possibility of statistical regression was minimized in the present design as: (a) All the students in a given college who had physical science as one of their methods courses were chosen. (b) Instruments used had reliability in the accepted range.

(v) Selection Bias

Random selection of colleges and random assignment of treatments maintained the equivalence between groups to the extent possible.

Threats to External Validity

If the experimental situation is over controlled, it becomes artificial and results become meaningless and inapplicable. The main threat to external validity arises from over control.

Since the experiment was conducted in the actual classroom conditions, threat to external validity arising from artificial laboratory conditions was at the minimum level.

(i) Interaction of Selection and Treatment

This was minimized because no scope was given for voluntary assignment of subjects and samples were drawn from typical teacher education colleges.

(ii) Hawthorne Effect and Artificiality of Experimental Setting

The present study minimized the effect due to these variables by conducting the treatments in the actual classroom, during regular class hours, and by utilizing the services of the respective teacher educators. This ensured normalcy of treatment procedures.

(iii) Interaction Effect of Testing

The use of a pre-test was avoided in order to conceal the purpose of the experiment. The student teachers were exposed to training without being aware of the purpose of the experiment.

SELECTION OF THE EXPERIMENTER

The science teacher educators of the four colleges randomly chosen were asked to provide the necessary training to the student teachers in their respective colleges. A panel of experts provided them with an orientation towards the model using the training approach suggested by Joyce and Weil (1978). This consisted of four components, namely:

(i) Describing and understanding the model.
(ii) Viewing the model.
(iii) Planning, and
(iv) Adopting the model.

Demonstration lessons were arranged and lesson plan formats were provided. The handout prepared (Appendix A & B) was also circulated.

TOOLS USED

The Four tools used in the study were:

(1) Willingness scale for teacher educators.
(2) Theories check up for student teachers.
(3) Reaction scale for student teachers.
(4) Willingness scale for student teachers.

Willingness Scale for Teacher Educators

To study the willingness of teacher educators, to implement models of teaching, Passi and Sansanwal (1985) developed a willingness scale. The original scale was a three-point scale and consisted of twenty-three items. Passi, *et al.*, administered the scale after a training schedule for teacher educators in models of teaching. The present study on teacher educators was a descriptive study, with an incidental sample. Hence the original scale was modified to suit the present study. A rough draft of items was prepared and a panel of judges to assess its suitability examined the tool.

Content validity refers to the degree to which the test actually measures or is specifically related to the traits for which it was designed. A panel of judges comprising of teacher educators of Centre for Education Research, Nagarjuna University (Guntur) was chosen. The panel judged its adequacy and some changes were suggested and they were incorporated.

The reliability was determined by using the technique of Split-Half method. The test was divided into two equivalent 'halves' and the correlation was found for the half tests. From the reliability of the half test, the correlation of the whole test was determined using the Spearman-Brown prophecy formula (Garret, 1985). The odd-even split method was used to split the test. The correlation co-efficient of the split half test was 0.61 and the reliability of the whole test was 0.757.

The tool finally used consisted (Appendix C) of sixteen items to be rated on a three point scale. Agree/Neutral/Disagree. The positive statements were scored as three for agree, two for neutral, and one for disagree. The negative items were scored as three for disagree, two for neutral, and one for agree. The maximum score one could earn was forty-eight.

Theory Check up for Student Teachers

After orienting students-teachers to models of teaching, it is necessary to check their theoretical understanding of the model. For this study, a theory check up test consisting of fourteen items was prepared. Twelve questions were of choosing the correct alternative type and two were of matching the correct response type. The maximum score that could be obtained was twenty-one (Appendix D).

The tool was first standardized. The content validity was ensured by having it examined by a panel of judges. Item analysis was done and only those with high discriminating value were retained. The reliability of scale was found out by using split-half method. The correlation co-efficient of Split-Half test was 0.72 and the reliability of the whole test was 0.83.

The final fourteen items test consisted of questions relating to all aspects of Inquiry Training Model, i.e., different phases of a model, Syntax of ITM, discrepant event types of questions asked, process of analysis and presentation of analogies (Appendix D) for the copy of the theory check up.

Reaction Scale for Student Teachers

The feasibility of any innovation depends on how the participants trained in it react towards it. Thus the necessity for measuring the reactions of the student teachers towards ITM was felt and a reaction scale was administered after training.

D'Lima and Sugandhi (1986) prepared a reaction scale consisting of twenty-three items to be rated on a five-point scale. The investigator made slight modifications in the original tool to suit the conditions of the present study.

The modified version of the tool was submitted to a panel of judges. The suggestions of the experts were used to incorporate some changes.

The reliability was measured using the even/odd - split-half technique. The correlation co-efficient of the split halves was 0.66 and the reliability co-efficient of the whole test was 0.795.

The final version consisting of twenty-three items to be rated on a three point scale: Agree/Neutral/Disagree was administered (Appendix E). The statements were scored as three for Agree, two for Neutral and one for Disagree for positive statements and vice versa for negative statements. The total score obtainable is forty-nine.

Willingness Scale for Student Teachers

Although theoretical understanding and reactions of the feasibility of 'Inquiry Training Models' it is very essential to find out how willing they are to implement models of teaching. D'Lima and Sugandhi developed a willingness questionnaire consisting of nine items. The scale was developed to find out the willingness of student teachers who had attended a workshop on ITM and CAM models of teaching.

The investigator adopted a modified version of the scale. The content validity was established using the expert opinion of a panel of judges. The reliability was measured by split-half technique. The co-efficient of split halves was found to be 0.704 and reliability co-efficient of the whole test was 0.83.

The final scale (see Appendix F) consisted of five items to be rated on a three point scale (willing) Yes/Undecided/Unwilling. The statements were all positive and were scored as three for willing, two for undecided and one for unwilling.

A Handout and Lesson Plan

The investigator keeping in view the psychological principles of motivation and interest prepared this. It comprises a description of models of teaching and its utility, ITM, phases in ITM and effects of ITM. The lesson plan describes the phases in ITM with an example of black bodies. Incorporating the suggestions of a panel of judges ensured the content validity.

DATA ANALYSIS TECHNIQUES

Teacher Educators Responses

The teacher educators' response data was gathered by using the willingness scale. The Chi-square test, which is a non-parametric test, was used to analyze the teacher educators' data. The score distributions were drawn and tested against equal distribution hypothesis. The Chi-square test represents a useful method of comparing experimentally obtained results with those to be expected theoretically on some hypothesis.

By adopting the scoring system already explained the individual scores for the teacher educators on the willingness scale were computed, classified and observed frequencies were arrived at.

To identify the influence of the selected variables on willingness scale scores for each sub-sample, means, and standard deviations were calculated for finding out the significance of difference between means, '*t*' test was applied and the mean difference tested for significance at 0.05 level.

Student Teachers Responses

For analysing the student teachers data with reference to the three tools the individual scores were arrived at.

'Simple Experiments Design' that involves one-way variance analysis was chosen. The investigator felt that the use of ANOVA technique would help in analysing the student teacher data and drawing conclusions about the superiority of training strategy. This is a situation where there are more than two means to be compared and where the significance of the differences among several means is desired. The means were uncorrelated measures of scores and one criterion of classification at a time is used. The ANOVA technique is applied to the theory check up scores, reaction scale scores and willingness scale scores.

In this chapter the research procedure adopted was described. The sampling procedures adopted and tools used were described. The procedure adopted for collecting the data and techniques used for analysing the data were explained. Chapter 4 presents the details of the plan and procedure that was used in this study.

Data Analysis, Discussion and Conclusions

INTRODUCTION

The concern of the present investigation was to identify the training needs of student teachers in the implementation of the models of teaching. One of the aims of the study was to assess the willingness of teacher educators to implement models of teaching. It also tried to find out the effectiveness of training strategies in terms of theoretical understanding of ITM, reaction towards ITM, and willingness to implement ITM of student teachers.

TEACHER EDUCATORS' RESPONSE TO WILLINGNESS SCALE

The willingness scale (Appendix C) was administered to the teacher educators. Individual scores were computed and classified. The distribution of scores was tested against equal probability hypothesis. Table 5.1 shows the distribution of scores among the three options: Agree, Neutral, and Disagree.

Table 5.1

Overall Response of Teacher Educators

Trait	*Agree*	*Neutral*	*Disagree*
Score Frequency	(41-48)	(25-40)	(16-24)
fe	17	17	17
fo	23	20	8

$\chi^2 = 7.4^*$ df= 2 χ^2 is significant at 0.05 level

It can be seen from Table 5.1, the teacher educators had shown a definite trend in favour of agreement. Overall reactions of teacher educators was positive. They had shown willingness to accept salient features and usefulness of models of teaching.

Teacher education programme is a place where constant research takes place. New innovative ideas surface from time to time. The very nature of teacher education programme allows for constant change. The curriculum is flexible and teacher educators generally are ready to accept change. In contrast, in the other disciplines, course structure is rigid and latest developments are seldom incorporated.

This type of attitude was evident in teacher educator's response. They displayed a positive disposition towards models of teaching. The teacher educators were given opportunities to attend various in service teacher education programmes. Obviously, they had made good use of the available opportunities. This had influenced their professional readiness to implement models to teaching.

The positive trend expressed by teacher educators necessitates the study whether the willingness scores across the subgroups are also positive. A detailed examination of the influencing variables was taken up to find out whether the subgroups also show the same trend as the whole group. Comparisons of willingness scores of subgroups is shown in Table 5.2.

Table 5.2

Mean Differences in Willingness Scores—Variable Wise

No	*Variables*		*n*	*Mean*	*S.D.*	*Mean difference*	S_{ED}	*t*
1	Sex	Women	29	35.9	2.9	0.7	1.05	0.7
		Men	22	36.6	4.1			
2.	Educational Qualification	Only PG.	35	35.8	3.8	2.6	0.96	2.7*
		M.Phil./Ph.D	16	38.4	2.86			
3.	Teaching Experience as Teacher Educator	> 10 years	37	36.7	3.78	1.3	0.95	1.4
		< 10 years	14	35.4	2.8			
4.	Courses Handled	Foundation courses	10	34.0	3.8	2.7	1.25	2.2*
		Methods Courses	41	36.7	2.2			
5.	In service Programme	Yes	34	36.2	4.1	1.9	0.87	2.2*
		No	17	34.3	2.1			

*** Denotes 't' values significant at 0.05 level**

It can be seen from Table 5.2, of the five variables chosen three variables seemed to be influencing the willingness scores. Sex and teaching experience of teacher educators were not influencing the willingness scores.

It can be seen that those who have done research on more scientific levels during M.Phil. and Ph.D. degree courses had a better chance of exposure to the latest developments. They may have had an orientation of innovations and also possible exposure towards models of teaching. Their access to journals and books might have led to their having more favourable attitudes than those who possess minimum basic qualifications like post-graduate degree only.

Attendance at in service programmes seems to have developed positive attitudes in teacher educators towards innovations. It may have provided them with a chance to keep abreast of latest developments. Thus in service programmes seemed to be influencing the teacher educators willingness scores.

Teacher educators who have handled methods courses are, probably, the ones who have more chances of getting exposure to new techniques and their implementation than those teaching foundation courses get. They train student teachers to adopt new techniques in their practice teaching sessions. In this endeavour they might have had access to adapt new strategies. Teachers of foundation courses were confined to their respective teaching disciplines that were, predominantly, theoretical in their orientation. This limitation seems to be influencing the willingness scores.

Both men and women have shown a similar response pattern to the willingness scale. They have indicated identical points of interest and have shown the same state of aptitude towards innovations. The non significant 't' value in Table 5.2 shows that the willingness scores of teacher educators does not have anything to do with the sex of teacher educators.

A teacher education programme by its very nature and scope does not provide for a differential aptitude of men over women or vice versa. The general apprehension that women are conservative and would not expose themselves to innovations was found to be false in this study. The experience as a teacher educator did not influence the trend of opinion expressed by them. The demands of their professional duties young or old compelled them from time to time to update their teaching competencies and communicative techniques.

Having established the willingness of teacher educators to implement models of teaching and also identifying the factors that affected the extent of willingness, the research extends itself to the item analysis of each item on the willingness scale.

An attempt was made to investigate the intensity of the overall responses on each of the items on the willingness scale. This is presented in Table 5.3.

Table 5.3

Item Wise Analysis of Teacher Educators' Response

No	*Opinion*	*Yes*	*Can't Say*	*No*	χ^2
1.	I have knowledge of models of teaching	45	2	4	69.3*
2.	I find the models of teaching are more effective than existing methods of teaching	43	4	4	59.6*
3.	I understand the theory underlying the models	37	6	8	35.4*
4.	I have faith in educational innovations	35	14	2	32.8*
5.	It is not difficult to implement models of teaching	12	14	25	5.8*
6.	Implementing models is not time consuming	25	10	16	6.7*
7.	Adequate facilities for implementing models are available in my institution	25	10	16	6.7*
8.	The instructional materials for implementing models of teaching are available	10	12	29	12.8*
9.	I can implement models of teaching in spite of several limitations	31	8	12	17.8*
10.	I am ready to implement models of teaching provided my work load is reduced	21	20	10	4.3
11.	The inclusion of models of teaching can improve teacher training programme.	41	8	2	51.9*
12.	Student teachers find it difficult to understand the theory of models of teaching	27	14	10	9.3*
13.	The use of models of teaching in teacher education curriculum is practicable	10	14	27	9.3*
14.	Implementation of models of teaching will have financial implications	14	20	17	1.1
15.	Models of teaching are not new as salient features are already found in existing methods	23	14	14	3.2
16.	Research on models of teaching should be disseminated for classroom teaching	29	14	8	13.8*

* Indicates χ^2 values that are significant at 0.05 level

The response of the teacher educators towards each statement was tested against equal probability hypothesis to identify the trend of opinions. It can be seen from Table 5.3, that there is a significant trend of opinion in teacher educators on thirteen of the sixteen statements on the willingness scale.

On the basis of the opinions expressed the following conclusions can be drawn.

The teacher educators reported that they have faith in innovations. This is supported by the fact that they had knowledge of models of teaching. They acknowledged the fact that models of teaching were more effective than traditional methods and admitted that the salient features of models were not found in the existing methods of teaching. They were predominantly of the opinion that implementation of models would improve teacher education programmes and there was a need for classroom dissemination of models of teaching.

In spite of admitting that they were ready to implement models of teaching, teacher educators found it impracticable to implement models of teaching. The trend of the opinions showed that they had a tendency of finding excuses when they had to implement new techniques. They felt that adequate facilities for implementing models were not available in their institutions.

The impediments they expected to face in the implementation of models were time constraints, inability of student teachers to comprehend the theory of the models, and lack of instructional materials.

Teacher educators believed that models of teaching are vehicles of communication of scientific process skills. They believed in the philosophy of models of teaching to develop strategies to improve teacher education programmes. But, they expressed that they had some difficulties in the implementation of the models, as they were preoccupied with many other practical activities and requirements at the same time.

The teacher educators did not have any firm opinion about the financial implications. They also were not very sure whether there was any similarity between the features in the models of teaching and traditional techniques of teaching. There is no trend in their opinions about the additional workload involved in teaching of models.

The teacher educators have expressed an intense positive trend of opinion towards three items. They have expressed confidence on models of teaching, have knowledge of models of teaching, and have acknowledged the fact that the inclusion of models of teaching can improve teacher education programme. These positive opinions have far reaching consequences as the inclusion of models of teaching primarily requires willingness of teacher educators to receive and experiment with the new techniques.

STUDENT TEACHERS' RESPONSE DATA

The 'Simple Methods Experiment' design was used to find out the effectiveness of training strategies developed for training student teachers in Inquiry Training Model. Two main categories of training strategies were identified.

(i) Small group approaches.
(ii) Large group approaches.

In each category, variations in training were introduced. The descriptions of various groups based on training strategy adopted are as follows:

Small Group Approaches

Group A: Only theoretical orientation group
Group B: Conventional teaching method group
Group C: Modular approach group

Large Group Approaches

Group D: Only theoretical orientation group
Group E: Conventional teaching method group
Group F: Modular approach group

Group A and Group D were given only theoretical orientation in the form of a hand out and lesson plan on ITM (Appendix A and B).

Group B and E were exposed to a lecture, demonstration and discussion sessions on ITM.

Group C and F were exposed to theoretical orientation in the form of a hand out. They were then exposed to a lecture–demonstration session. Finally, they took part in group discussion on ITM.

The teacher educators involved in the study were well oriented to conduct the experiment. For identifying the influence of training strategies the post test scores of the student teachers on the three dependent variables were analysed by adopting one-way analysis of variance of uncorrelated means.

STUDENT TEACHERS' RESPONSE TO THEORY CHECK UP

A tool to measure the understanding of student teachers of the various components and theoretical aspects of ITM was administered (Appendix D). The analysis of variance data of the three large group and three small groups strategies is presented in Tables 5.5 and 5.6.

Group A, B, and C, whose sample size was between fifteen and twenty, were exposed to three training strategies. Variations in training strategies were provided to the three groups. The analysis of variance (ANOVA) is shown in Table 5.4.

Table 5.4

ANOVA Table: Theory Check Up - Training Strategies

Groups	*A*	*B*	*C*	*Whole Group*
n	17	18	15	Σ n = 50
x	201	232	197	Grand Σ x = 630
$\bar{x}$	11.8	12.9	13.1	Grand Mean= 12.63
x^2	1838	3361	2964	Grand Σ x^2 = 8163

Summary: Analysis of Variance

Source of Variations	*df*	*Sum of squares*	*Mean Square variance*	*F*
Among the means of conditions	2	16.8	8	1.8
Within conditions	47	209	4.4	

F = 1.8 not significant at 0.05 level.

The result of the analysis of variance on theory check up scores on the 'small group' student teachers revealed that there were not significant variations. It means that whatever be the training strategy the student teachers understanding of the model is nearly the same.

The choice of small sample size was made with the assumption that it would provide impressive individual exposure to student teachers. The modular approach was expected to give intense type of treatment. But these assumptions were not upheld in the case of theoretical understanding of student teachers. Mere exposure to the handout and a lesson plan (Appendix A and B) could also produce the same degree of understanding of ITM.

The class size of physical science methods course is generally fifty to seventy-five students. Keeping the ground realities in view, the training strategies were tried out on three large groups. Table 5.5 shows the analysis of variance results of training strategies on large groups.

Table 5.5

ANOVA Table: Theory Check Up - Teaching Strategies

GROUPS	*D*	*E*	*F*	*WHOLE GROUP*
n	57	75	51	Σn = 183
x	798	982	766	Grand Σ x = 2546
$\bar{x}$	14	13.1	15	Grand Mean = 14
x^2	13648	14654	12106	Grand Σ x^2 = 40408

Summary: Analysis of Variance

Source of variations	*df*	*Sum of squares*	*Mean square variance*	*F*
Among the means of conditions	2	113.3	56.6	
Within conditions	180	4873.3	27.1	2.1

F = 2.1 which is not significant at 0.05 level.

In the large groups, Table 5.5 revealed those training strategies did not produce significant differences in the theory check up scores of student teachers. It can be seen that whatever be the training strategy, the understanding of the student teachers was of the same level.

In the case of large groups also there was no significant variations between groups exposed to mere theoretical orientation, conventional teaching or modular approach. This was contradictory to the assumption that modular approach would produce better understanding of the concepts and implications of ITM.

The elaborate training provided in modular approach comprised of group work in addition to theoretical orientation and lecture demonstration. But it could not produce a significant increase in theoretical cognition compared to the other two groups.

The research tried to find out if there were significant differences between the large and small groups in their theoretical understanding. Table 5.6 shows the ANOVA between large group means and small group means on theory check up.

The non-significant F value indicates that the treatment was uniformly received. Sample size did not influence the theory check up scores of student teachers. This could be attributed to the novelty of the method. The interest generated has cut across the numbers, and has succeeded in pushing the type of training strategy to the background.

Table 5.6
ANOVA Table: Large Group <> Small Group:
Theory Check Up Scores

Groups	*Small*	*Large*	*Whole group*
n	50	183	Σ n = 233
x	630	2546	Grand Σ x = 3176
$\bar{x}$	12.6	14	Grand Mean= 13.3
x^2	8163	40408	Grand Σx^2 = 48571

Summary: Analysis of Variance

Source of Variations	*Df*	*Sum of squares*	*Mean Square variance*	*F*
Among the means of conditions	1	67.7	67.7	3.8
Within conditions	231	4371.9	18.9	

F = 3.8 which is not significant at 0.05 level.

It could be concluded that the inherent features of the model have arrested the attention of student teachers. Hence they have eagerly tried to assimilate various components of the model. This has finally led to a high theoretical cognition of the student teachers.

It was interesting to find out that only ten per cent of the student teachers had scored low scores on the theory check up. The research extends further to find out how the students have responded to each of the items on the theory check up. Item wise response to each item on the theory check up is presented in Table 5.7.

The student teachers responses to the theory check up shows that they understood very well the meaning of the terms; inquiry and discrepant event. The interest in the model has made them to identify the person (Richard Suchman) who devised this model. They have acquired sound knowledge of the type of questions to be asked and the classroom climate of the inquiry sessions, they have also identified the instructional effects of ITM.

Table 5.7
Item Wise Distribution of Student Teachers Response to Theory Check Up

Sl. No.	*Responses to given questions*	*No. of Correct Responses*	*No. of Incorrect Responses*
1.	Inquiry means to investigate and solve a problem	187	46
2.	A discrepant event is an unexpected event	176	57
3.	Inquiry Training model was designed by Richard Suchman	207	26
4.	An Inquiry training class requires active Participation by all students	187	46
5.	In ITM students gather data by questioning (Yes/No type questions)	178	55
6.	Students gather data by asking questions which are answerable by 'Yes' or 'No' Suchman rule	171	62
7.	The correct response of a teacher in an inquiry class is Now let us analyze your questions why did you ask '— — —' question?	123	110
8.	The ITM is oriented towards the development of scientific process skills and creativity	180	53
9.	An inquiry session ends only after analysis of inquiry session is made	68	165
10.	A science teacher wants students, to know why people prefer to wear cotton clothes in summer is an example suitable for inquiry lesson	154	79
11.	What material is used to make the objects? An inappropriate question in an inquiry session	102	131
12.	Development of scientific process skills is an instructional effect of ITM?	105	128

Match the Following

(a)

S. No.	*Stage number*	*Name of Stage*	*Correct*	*Incorrect*
a.	One	Syntax		
b.	Two	Principles of reaction	102	131
c.	Three	Social System		
d.	Four	Support System		

(b)

S.No.	Phase No	Phase	Correct	Incorrect
1.	One	Enocounter with the problem		
2.	Two	Data gathering—verification		
3.	Three	Data gathering-—experimentation	114	119
4.	Four	Formulation of an explanation		
5.	Five	Analysis of inquiry process		

Though they have acquired the knowledge of technique used for data gathering (Yes/No Questions), but in effect, they failed to apply the same in a subsequent question. They were not able to find out the inappropriate question among the four questions. The particular question which had reference to the type of material used could not meet the Yes/No answer requirement.

The general teaching session ends when an explanation is given to a problem. This model requires an analysis of the data gathering phase and stating of analogies for the session to end. The students have shown a lack of knowledge of concluding the inquiry session.

But an encouraging response was that they could pick out the discrepant event from the four choices in which three choices were not suitable for ITM. The students have gained a thorough knowledge of ITM and its ramifications.

In the two questions on matching the phases of syntax of ITM, and phases of a model with phase number the response shows that they have not understood the steps. They have not grasped the hierarchical order of the stages of ITM.

The theoretical knowledge acquired by student teachers is high but they have not shown equal comprehension of the steps to be followed. Training in asking pin pointed questions has to be given. The student teachers require practice to comprehend the phases. By and large, the achievement of the student teachers who were exposed to ITM for the first time was praiseworthy.

STUDENT TEACHERS RESPONSE TO REACTION SCALE

The student teachers were administered a reaction scale (Appendix E) after the training schedule was completed. The reaction scores were computed and tabulated. The analysis of variance of the three large groups and three small groups and between the two types of groups is presented in Tables 5.8, 5.9, and 5.10.

In Table 5.8 the analysis of variance of reaction scores of small groups is presented.

Table 5.8

ANOVA For Response of Small Groups to Reaction Scale

Groups	*A*	*B*	*C*	*Whole group*
n	17	18	15	Σ n =50
x	872	982	840	Grand Σ = 2694
$\bar{x}$	51.3	54.5	56	Grand Mean= 53.9
x^2	46952	53906	45264	Grand Σ x^2 = 146122

ANOVA Summary

Source of variations	*df*	*Sum of squares*	*Mean Square variance*	*F*
Among the means of conditions	2	189.3	94.6	5.7*
Within conditions	47	780.7	16.6	

F = 5.7* Significant at 0.05 level.

The results of the reaction scores of the student teachers revealed a significant variation in the small groups, the tendency being a weightage towards the modular group 'C'. It could be seen that favourable reactions could be expected by imparting training through the module approach in comparison to training approaches.

The modular approach group in addition to the theoretical orientation and lecture demonstration session had group work in the end. They divided into groups of three to four students. They prepared a lesson plan of a topic in physical science. Each group leader presented the discrepant event. The group discussion helped to clarify the doubts. They discussed threadbare each other's presentation. This has led to the significant positive reaction that student teachers have shown in comparison to the other two training strategies.

During the group work in Group C the following example was presented as a discrepant event. A student took two beakers of a liquid. He passed a colourless gas through both of them. In one of the beakers, the water turned milky and in the other it was clear. Why do you think this happened?

In the group discussion the following interesting observations were made: If students are not aware of the nature of gases and in particular properties of carbon dioxide they would not solve it. At the most, they might identify the differences in nature of gases. If students are aware of the properties of carbon dioxide, they might identify it immediately. Hence, they decided that it would not be a discrepant event.

But on further discussion they said that students could investigate into the discrepancy by verifying the nature of liquid, experimentation technique, and nature of gases. When they would identify that the discrepancy is because of the gases passed, they would be supplied with a fact sheet, which would enable them to identify the gas.

The group was of the opinion that this event should be demonstrated for better understanding. This sort of discussion has made the student teachers develop a positive reaction towards the model. They have found it to be useful and a better technique than conventional teaching followed in the schools.

The research tried to find out the reaction trend of student teachers that were grouped as large samples. Table 5.9 shows the ANOVA computations for large group samples trained by different strategies.

Table 5.9

ANOVA for Response of Large Group Student Teachers to Reaction Scale

Groups	D	E	F	*Whole group*
n	57	75	51	$\Sigma n = 183$
x	2982	4215	3012	Grand $\Sigma x = 10209$
$\bar{x}$	52.3	56.2	59.1	Grand Σ Mean= 55.9
x^2	159972	178684	2964	Grand $\Sigma x^2 = 577073$

ANOVA Summary

Source of variations	df	Sum of squares	Mean Square variance	F
Among the means of conditions	2	1245.6	622.8	17.8*
Within conditions	180	6299	35	

F = 17.8*, which is significant at 0.05 level.

The significant F value indicates that there is an influence of training strategy on the reaction scores, which has produced significant variations in the scores. The trend was in favour of the modular approach training strategy.

The additional exposure in the modular group was the group work. The sample of fifty-seven students divided themselves into eight groups of seven students each. Each group prepared a lesson plan and had group discussions.

One group presented the following interesting discrepant event. The student teachers had a long brain storming type of session before they could finally arrive at the explanation for the problem.

The event is as follows: A teacher took a wooden block A. Over it he sprinkled some water and placed a beaker B on it (made of some good conductor). He poured a liquid C into the beaker and dipped a tube into it. A stream of air was blown into the beaker. After some time he noticed that the water on the wooden block froze and the beaker stuck to the block.

The first reaction was that discrepant event would be easily understood if it was demonstrated.

The questions were about 'A' the block, 'B' the beaker, and 'C' the liquid. There were some irrelevant questions like did you introduce ice on the sly? May be you had stuck ice to the bottom of the beaker?

Some others said that they would not accept it as they thought it was not a true situation. This exercise really led to a wide ranging animated discussion. This sort of interaction made them come face to face with the various phases of inquiry process. They were enthralled by the method and this contributed to their positive reactions.

In both, the small group and large group samples, the modular approach produced significant positive reactions. It was attempted to find out if the variations between the large groups and small group training strategies were significant.

Table 5.10 shows the F test computations for variance between small and large group reaction scores.

Table 5.10

Anova For Large Group <> Small Group Reaction Scores

Groups	D	E	Whole group
n	50	183	n = 233
x	2694	10209	Grand Σ x = 12903
$\bar{x}$	53.9	55.9	Grand Mean= 54.9
x^2	146122	577073	Grand x^2 = 723195

Summary of ANOVA

Source of variations	*df*	*Sum of squares*	*Mean Square variance*	*F*
Among the means of conditions	1	142.8	142.8	3.9*
Within conditions	231	8513.8	36.8	

F = 3.9 which is not significant at 0.05 level.

The non-significant F value indicates that the reaction scores didn't depend on the group size of student teachers. The positive reaction generated by the inherent attributes of ITM was not hindered by the fact that the student teacher was part of a group of fifteen or part of a group of over fifty.

The only criteria that mattered was the type of training where modular approach was best received. Only ten percent of the student teachers had shown negative reaction. Therefore, a further attempt was made to find out the reactions of student teachers on each of the items of the reaction scale.

Table 5.11 shows the distribution of the whole sample response to the three-point reaction scale, item wise.

In all the twenty-three statements, the students have shown agreement with the positive statement and disagreement with the negative statements.

They have shown a recognizable positive trend towards ITM and its efficacy. They have shown wide scale acceptance that ITM can develop science process skills. They have shown acceptance to the fact that ITM develops creative thinking of children. They believed that ITM makes students alert and attentive. Four out of the six groups, B, C, E, F were exposed to lecture demonstration sessions. The example was on heat transfer. The discrepant event presented was that Anita poured tea into four teacups. Three of the four cups broke but the fourth teacup did not break. Why did you think this happened?

Each group asked nearly twenty to twenty-five questions before arriving at the explanation. The questions were as diverse as: Did someone push them down? Was some chemical added to the tea?

A student teacher had the following explanation to offer when analysis of the inquiry session was made. The three teacups were in unstable equilibrium position (tilted) and the fourth was in stable equilibrium (flat, upright). On pouring tea, they further tilted, and fell down, and broke.

Table 5.11

Item Wise Response Distribution of Student Teachers Reactions to Reaction Scale

S. No	*Response*	*Agree*	*Neutral*	*Disagree*
1.	I find it difficult to formulate a discrepant event	107	74	50
2.	I think it is difficult to understand the process of pupils through this model	70	42	119
3.	A teacher will be more active while teaching through ITM compared to ordinary teaching	187	27	17
4.	Creative thinking of children can be stimulated through this model of	205	19	7
5.	It is suited to the present class room setting 60 to 70 students	111	49	71
6.	It makes pupils alert and attentive	206	20	5
7.	I do not feel competent to handle various phases of the model	52	70	109
8.	The model teaches pupils not to respond without thinking	181	25	25
9.	This model teaches pupils to view a situation from various angles	217	10	4
10.	This model develops the spirit of scientific inquiry among students	192	26	13
11.	There is a chance of pupil getting frustrated when they are not able to find the solution	65	58	108
12.	It discourages the pupils from thinking that theirs is the only right answer	136	45	50
13.	Strict adherence to the rules of the model destroys the pupils creative spirit	35	43	153
14.	It is time consuming, yet there is no thorough understanding of the subject matter	44	42	145
15.	This model gives a sense of participation to each child	190	21	20
16.	This model is not suited to the present day school curriculum	141	49	41
17.	It discourages rote learning	184	22	25
18.	The model teaches pupils to delay conclusions	138	45	48
19.	The model teaches pupils to ask pinpointed questions	172	28	31
20.	Discipline in the classroom cannot be maintained while using this model	85	99	47
21.	This model provides freedom to student for independent thinking	197	25	9
22.	Implementation of this model requires a change in examination system	178	36	17
23.	This model requires resourceful teachers	172	39	20

Yet another reasoned that there was manufacturing defect; another student teacher wanted to know if the material of handle, base tray or the material of teacups was different.

This sort of diverse thought made them to agree with the items about the development of independent thinking, the ability to view a situation from various angles. They agreed in large numbers that ITM discourages students from thinking that theirs is the only right answer.

The demonstration or group work was done in the general classroom setting. Hence, they were positive in their reaction that this model is suited to the present classroom setting of sixty to seventy students. But they feel that there is a need to modify the curriculum to incorporate models of teaching. They have expressed the need to bring about changes in the examination system that is generally confined to measuring only understanding in the cognitive domain only. This is amply supported by the fact that they have agreed that ITM discourages rote learning.

They have recognized the fact that teachers are very active while teaching through this model and that it requires resourceful teachers to implement ITM.

Two reactions of student teachers need to be carefully analysed. They have admitted that they were finding it difficult to formulate a discrepant event. This means that they require a little more practice with which they would be able to convert most of the cause-effect relationships into discrepant events.

The second is about the inability to handle the various phases of the models, this is in line with the lack of understanding they have shown in the phases of the models of teaching. Giving sufficient practice may solve this difficulty expressed.

By and large, the reaction shown by the student teachers is positive. They have understood the various advantages of the model. This is a very encouraging response that on the whole they are having a positive reaction towards ITM.

STUDENT TEACHERS' RESPONSE TO WILLINGNESS SCALE

After completion of training, a willingness scale (Appendix F) was administered to the student teachers. Their willingness scores were computed. It was attempted to find out whether willingness scores depended on the training strategy or the sample size. Tables 5.12, 5.13, 5.14 show the analysis of variance of willingness scores with respect to variations in sample size and treatment strategy adopted.

Table 5.12 is the data of analysis of variance of willingness scores of small groups.

Table 5.12

ANOVA for Response of Small Groups to Willingness Scale

Groups	*A*	*B*	*C*	*Whole group*
n	17	18	15	$\Sigma n = 50$
x	185	212	188	Grand $\Sigma x = 11.7$
$\bar{x}$	10.9	11.8	12.5	Grand Mean= 585
x^2	1963	2162	2900	Grand $\Sigma x^2 = 7025$

Anova Summary

Source of variations	*df*	*Sum of squares*	*Mean Square variance*	*F*
Among the means of conditions	2	21.95	11	3.3*
Within conditions	47	158.60	3.3	

F = 3.3 * which is significant at 0.05 level.

From Table 5.12, the major finding is that there is a significant variation in the willingness scores of students belonging to small groups. The students who were imparted training using 'modular approach' were having higher willingness scores than those who were exposed to either conventional or theoretical orientation strategies.

The student teachers of Group C exposed to modular approach were given intense treatment. The group discussion made them to identify the salient features of ITM. They were able to find out in detail each aspect of the model. The merits of the model were so clearly observed that they were very willing to implement models of teaching.

The large group willingness scores were analysed to find out if their willingness was influenced by the training strategies. Table 5.13 shows the ANOVA computations for large group response to willingness scale.

Table 5.13

ANOVA for Large Group Response to Willingness Scale

Groups	D	E	F	*Whole group*
n	57	75	51	Σ n = 183
x	615	928	668	Grand Σ x = 2211
$\overline{x}$	10.7	12.3	13.1	Grand Σ Mean= 12
x^2	6891	11928	8840	Grand Σ x^2 = 27659

ANOVA Summary

Source of variations	*df*	*Sum of squares*	*Mean Square variance*	*F*
Among the means of conditions	2	154.2	77.1	17.5*
Within conditions	180	791.5	4.4	

F = 17.5* which is significant at 0.05 level.

Table 5.13 revealed that there is a significant difference in the willingness of student teachers exposed to different training strategies. Those who were exposed to training module approach showed more willingness to implement ITM.

The student teachers trained by modular approach showed more willingness than other groups. This could be attributed to the type of training received. The group work involved presentation of the discrepant event prepared by them. Logical enlightened arguments and discussion marked the group discussions.

This sort of activity has made them to identify the salient features and utility of the model. This has led to the high willingness scores shown by this group.

The next aspect was whether the class size would have an effect on the willingness scores. Table 5.14 shows the ANOVA between large groups and small groups.

Table 5.14 shows the variations among the groups with respect to the sample size.

Table 5.14

Anova Table: Large Group <> Small Group Willingness Scores

Groups	*Small*	*Large*	*Whole group*
n	50	183	Σ n = 233
x	585	2211	Grand Σ x = 2796
$\bar{x}$	11.7	12	Grand Mean= 11.9
Σx^2	7025	27659	Grand Σx^2 = 34684

ANOVA Summary

Source of variations	*df*	*Sum of squares*	*Mean Square variance*	*F*
Among the means of conditions	1	5.72	5.72	1.01*
Within conditions	231	1307.2	5.66	

F = 1.01 is not significant at 0.05 level.

From Table 5.14 it could be seen that the sample size did not affect the willingness scores. There was no variation in the scores between large groups and small groups.

The student teachers actively participated in the lecture demonstration and group work. They were so engrossed in the activity that the number of students present in the class didn't effect them. They were, obviously, impressed by the novelty of the method and its salient features they were more than willing to use this model of teaching.

To find out how they have responded on each item on the willingness scale, item analysis was attempted. The sample distribution on the willingness scale is shown on Table 5.15. (Where Y - Yes, U - Undecided, N - No.)

Table 5.15

Item Wise Willingness of Student Teachers

Statement	*Y*	*U*	*N*
1. Are you ready to use the model in your practice teaching even if it is not insisted upon by your college supervisor?	125	64	42
2. Will you continue this model even if your first inquiry fails?	112	60	71
3. Will you use this model when you become a regular teacher?	137	64	32
4. Would you like to learn other models of teaching?	200	20	13
5. Would you encourage regular teachers to undergo training in ITM?	188	19	26

The student teachers have shown that they are willing to use ITM. The interest generated in learning about ITM has made them to agree to learn about other models of teaching. They are ready to advocate the utility of this model to others.

They are prepared to use ITM even if their first attempt to teach fails and continue to use ITM in their practice teaching.

DISCUSSION

The teacher educators had shown a tremendous willingness to implement models of teaching as revealed in the study. B.K. Passi, *et al.* (1989) in their study on teacher educators also reported that teacher educators were willing to implement the models of teaching if some support system was available.

The study undertaken by J.B. Valand (1983) tried to analyze the innovative proneness of teacher educators. He reported that variables such as age, sex, experience, academic qualifications, and in service education were significantly correlated with innovative proneness of teacher educators.

In a similar study conducted on teachers K.C. Gulati (1980) found that age, sex, and experience did not influence their innovative proneness. But, he found that those teachers who were professionally satisfied were more innovative prone.

In the present study age, sex, and teaching experience were not influencing the criterion measures. But professional qualifications, type of courses handled, and in service education did influence the willingness scores.

As seen in the responses of student teachers to theory check up and reaction scale, the students of the modular approach group were significantly showing greater readiness to implement models of teaching than the other two groups irrespective of the sample size.

One of the training strategies adopted was mere theoretical orientation in the form of a hand out. The hand out comprised of description of a model of teaching and its utility. The different types of models were briefly described. It also contained a brief description of the ITM and its phases. There was a detailed lesson plan with a physical science example on Black Bodies.

This handout has proved to be very useful in developing theoretical understanding of ITM. The theoretical understanding of the modular approach group is nearly the same as that of the theoretical orientation group.

We can conclude that modular approach is an effective strategy to train student teachers in the use of ITM. The group work and group discussion have played an important role in increasing the students' interest towards the model. It has helped them to get an idea of the various phases of the model. Probably an experience of classroom implementation of ITM might make them aware of all the inherent qualities of the model and lead to better understanding.

The questions asked during group discussion showed how sharply and divergently the student teachers were thinking. During the group work in Group F some of the examples quoted were:

(a) Two boys were on a trekking expedition. They stopped at their base camps. They started cooking and boiled eggs. The egg of one boy boiled but that of the other was par boiled though the time taken for boiling was the same. Why?
(b) In an apartment block, there were five apartments in a floor. There was an interesting cricket match relay on the television. In four houses they could receive the telecast, but in the fifth house they got a blurred reception, could you tell me why this happened?
(c) Two boys were playing near a railway track. Suddenly one boy exclaimed that he could hear the sound of a train approaching. The second boy agreed but took some time to respond. Why did a time lag exist between the two boys' responses?

The student teachers could identify discrepant events in all topics of physics, viz., sound, light, magnetism, etc., and chemistry, viz., electrolysis, metallurgy, etc. In the process of discussion, they could identify inappropriate questions. They were able to discard some examples and reframe some others to make them discrepant. The whole exercise was carried out in a cordial and enthusiastic mood.

Thus the reaction and willingness scores of modular approach group are significantly higher than those of the other two groups.

B.K. Passi, *et al.* (1985) also undertook a study to find out effectiveness of variations in training strategies for ITM in terms of understanding, competence, reaction, and willingness of student teachers.

The major conclusions reported are that both the groups understood the theoretical aspects to the same extent and the competence attained was of the same degree. Students of both groups had equally favourable reactions. This is similar to the conclusion of the present study that student teachers are favourable towards ITM.

Bhagaban, Subudhi (1991) also provided variations in training by varying demonstration and peer practice feedback. His technique was similar to micro teaching cycles. He also reported that in theoretical understanding and reactions the groups were identical. There was a significant difference in the skill of teaching competency as measured on TAG. Though the method of training adopted is different from the present study, it is significant to note that training strategy adopted did not affect theoretical understanding.

D'Lima and Lobo (1985) studied the effect of training strategy (consisted of theory-cum-demonstration) ITM. They divided the students into two groups based on their abstract reasoning ability. They reported that the student teachers showed a sound theoretical understanding. The results showed that the group with high abstract reasoning did not find it difficult to understand the puzzling problem. The groups high on theoretical understanding and high on abstract reasoning felt that the model is conducive to development of scientific process skills. The student teachers in the present study also acknowledged that ITM develops scientific process skills.

D'Lima and Sugandhi (1986) tried to find out the intellectual and emotional responses of the trainees towards ITM. The mean theoretical understanding scores were less than that reported by D'Lima and Lobo but the mean scores were higher than the expected chance score a subject could earn.

The abstract reasoning ability of a student teacher did not influence his theoretical understanding of ITM. They found variations in responses to the reaction scale scores between the groups which were high on abstract reasoning and low on abstract reasoning. The student teachers were willing to use the model even if they were not insisted upon. This sort of willingness was expressed by the student teachers trained by modular approach in the present study also.

Kamlesh Chaudary (1986) used a skill-based approach to train student teachers in models of teaching. He used the micro teaching approach. He reported that it was feasible to train student teachers using skill-based approach. He found that the student teachers teaching competency improved and they could use the model in their practice teaching. The present study did not attempt skill-based training keeping the time constraints and other difficulties involved in the implementation.

CONCLUSIONS

The teacher education programme should be one that satisfies the needs of the modern day schools. It is the responsibility of teacher educators to prepare science teachers who are conversant of the latest innovations. Models of teaching are examples of latest developments in the field of education whose knowledge would improve the teaching competence of student teachers. ITM could prove to be a very important tool in the hands of a resourceful teacher in teaching of science.

The present study has elicited the response of teacher educators to a willingness scale. The response pattern led to the conclusion that teacher educators are overwhelmingly in favour of models of teaching.

The teacher educators have fully realized the importance of the models of teaching and hence have shown a positive orientation to receive and implement the innovations. This is more conspicuously seen in the methods teachers, teaching physical science among other methods where a direct application of ITM was felt practicable.

While the majority of teacher educators had shown willingness to use models of teaching, those with added scholastic experience in the form of acquiring higher qualifications like M.Phil. and Ph.D. has displayed more positive disposition. Those teacher educators who had attended in service programmes had access to latest literature and exposure to innovations. Hence they had shown more willingness than those who had confined themselves to their regular professional duties only.

Inquiry skill training is one of the chief aims of science teaching. The knowledge of ITM is a necessity for every prospective teacher especially for those teaching science. ITM is concerned with the development of Inquiry Skills. Inquiry based teaching can be introduced in schools only if there are teachers trained to implement it. The training needs to begin at the teacher education level. The first recipients are the student teachers.

In this study student teachers were trained by three different strategies. One strategy was providing them only theoretical orientation. They were supplied with a hand out. The exposure to handout could also produce the same understanding of ITM on par with that produced by modular approach and conventional teaching. The novelty, variety and suspense of presentation of discrepant event in ITM evoked and sustained the same degree of interest across different presentations—theoretical, conventional and modular.

The handout was prepared on psychological principles. It has sustained the interest of student teachers and motivated them to read through the entire contents. The contents of the hand out were: the descriptions of models of teaching and its utility; the different families of models; description of ITM and its phases. It also had a detailed lesson plan with a physical science example on black bodies. The hand out ensured conceptual understanding of ITM.

One of the main goals of science teaching is to develop process skills. Inquiry training approach helps in developing the skills of creative thinking, scientific inquiry, divergent thinking, and independent thinking. The student teachers have shown positive trend towards ITM and its efficacy. Their reactions show that they have acknowledged the fact that ITM develops science process skills.

On the whole, reactions shown by student teachers indicate that they have understood the advantages of the model. It is very encouraging to observe that they are having a positive reaction towards ITM which when cultivated further would yield significant dividends.

The implementation of ITM requires the willingness of student teachers to use the model. The method and its salient features impressed the student teachers and they were willing to use ITM. They were motivated to learn other models.

The modular approach has been proved to be an effective strategy to train student teachers in the use of ITM. The modular approach comprises of three parts: (i) The theoretical orientation in the form of a handout, (ii) Lecture demonstration session, and (iii) Group work and Group discussion.

The lecture-demonstration session provided a practical and intimate training. The student teachers were the subjects and they tried to account for the discrepancy in the problem presented by the teacher educators. They had a real experience of ITM in session. The teacher educators were experienced and could provide an enthralling experience to the student teachers.

The final session of group work was very useful in helping student teachers to formulate discrepant events. The student teachers could formulate examples suitable for ITM in nearly all topics of physical science. The group discussion that completed the modular approach training strategy further augmented the understanding of different steps of ITM. The misconceptions were cleared and remedies were suggested.

The two additional factors over and above the information given in the handout used greater receptiveness and even instilled required skills in implementation of ITM towards maximizing effective science teaching.

The large group samples have shown understanding, positive reactions and willingness comparable to small groups. Hence ITM can be easily introduced in teacher education programme using modular approach training strategy. The inclusion of models of teaching in the curriculum can be recommended because there is approval from both teacher educators and student teachers. In service training for teacher educators to follow the phases of the model, to prepare lesson plans, and to prepare instructional materials is necessary. This will keep the teacher educators ready to implement as and when models are included in the curriculum.

Executive Summary

The Problem and its Significance

Education of secondary teachers is more than a hundred years old. During this period, the concept of teacher education has changed tremendously. Yet, some defects and shortcomings have been identified by different educationists such as: Artificiality of courses (both Theory and Practice); Ineffective methods of teaching; Less emphasis on the development of professional attitude; No impact on school practice; Lack of infrastructure; Poor economic background of student teachers.

Teacher education programmes have deep-rooted foundations in the Herbartian method. The climate in teacher education colleges is not generally research oriented. They work in isolation of the school system. There is seldom any interaction between research centres, teacher education colleges, and schools. The net result is that research is not percolating to the colleges of education. The school system changes according to the needs of the society and these needs reach the education colleges with a time lag.

The various aspects in the teacher education programmes have to be studied. The results may be used to analyze and suggest remedies in the following areas:

(i) Student teacher behaviour
(ii) Conceptual framework for a sound theory of instruction
(iii) Skill training and techniques of instruction to be given to student teachers
(iv) Use of innovations—classroom dissemination and teacher training strategies.

Some of the innovations that could be part of teacher education programmes are: Simulation, Microteaching, Team teaching, Programmed instruction, Interaction analysis, and Models of teaching.

The need of the hour is to motivate teacher educators towards implementation of innovations. They need to have a positive outlook towards new developments. The teacher educators have to be ready to be innovative. For achieving such a goal, training in models of teaching may pave the path. There is a long felt need to carry out programmes which will orient teacher educators to use better modes of student teacher programme.

In U.S.A., Joyce and Weil (1992) have done monumental work in the field of models of teaching. Models are highly specific teaching strategies designed to accomplish certain goals. Models of teaching are based on the empirical work, theories, and research of various people who worked in different fields. Joyce and Weil have developed more than twenty models of teaching and grouped them into four families based on their chief emphasis and the way they approach educational means and goals. In a developing country it is the duty of the teacher to stimulate the spirit of inquiry in the minds of the wards he cares for. Ability to stimulate the spirit of scientific inquiry is undoubtedly a valuable tool in the hands of an intelligent, an imaginative, and a responsible teacher. He initiates a student to scientific approach, systematic analysis, and problem solving, thus enlightening his mind and making him a responsible thinking citizen.

The Inquiry Training Model as developed by Suchman is classified under the information processing models of teaching by Joyce and Weil (1992). Suchman assumes that human beings are basically curious and problem solvers by nature. Suchman and his associates tried to analyze the methods employed by creative research personnel, especially physical scientists. They identified elements of inquiry process and devised the Inquiry Training Model.

Models of teaching have to gain acceptance from three groups: teacher educators, student teachers, and teachers at school level. This leads to the question of the training needs of the three groups.

As a beginning this study was undertaken on Inquiry Training Model. The knowledge of ITM is an absolute necessity for every prospective teacher especially those teaching science since ITM is concerned with the development of inquiry skills.

Concerns of the Study

The three important research questions that were raised in the present study:

1. Are the teacher educators willing to implement models of teaching?
2. What would be the training strategy that is suitable to train student teachers to use ITM?
3. What would be the response of the student teachers—the ultimate beneficiaries to the training provided?

The present study was undertaken to evolve training strategies to train student teachers to use Inquiry Training Model. The relative effectiveness of different training strategies were analysed in terms of three dependent variables:

(i) Theoretical understanding of ITM
(ii) Reaction towards ITM
(iii) Willingness to implement ITM

Objectives of the Study

For the purpose of practically verifying the propositions in the area of the study, the following were the objectives of the study.

1. To find out the willingness of the teacher educators to implement Models of Teaching.
2. To develop training strategies with variations in sample size and in treatment Variables, i.e., lecture demonstration theoretical orientation and group discussion.
3. To find out the effectiveness of training strategies in terms of student teachers
   (i) Theoretical understanding
   (ii) Reaction towards model
   (iii) Willingness to implement the model

Most of the studies reviewed are on classroom implementation of models of teaching. Control group/experimental group-parallel group design were adopted. The studies have shown that inquiry teaching was superior to conventional teaching in developing scientific process skills.

The studies reviewed on pre service teacher education on models of teaching have shown that training was generally provided by using the micro teaching approach. Generally, a pre test/post test single group or parallel group design was adopted. The studies have generally pointed out to the receptiveness of student teachers towards training. The review was useful in deciding the aims, method adopted, and procedure used in the present investigation.

Research Methodology

The present study comprises both descriptive and experimental type of research. It was descriptive to the extent that the willingness of teacher educators to implement models of teaching was found out through a normative survey willingness scale. The study is experimental to the extent that an attempt was made to manipulate the responses of student teachers by providing variations in training. A logical association between training strategies and observed respondent effects was attempted.

An incidental sample of fifty-one teacher educators from among the eighty teacher educators representing different teaching faculties of the nine teacher education colleges of Nagarjuna University were chosen.

Two hundred and thirty-three student teachers representing four out of the nine teacher education colleges of Nagarjuna University were chosen for the 'Simple Methods Experiment'. The colleges were chosen by a draw of lots and treatments were assigned to the groups also by a draw of lots.

Lewis (1968) has explicitly described the 'Simple Methods Experiment' design used. Kerlinger (1973) described it as 'one way analysis of variance' design.

The training strategies were divided into two groups depending on the sample size:

(i) Small group approaches (n = 15 to n = 20)
(ii) Large group approaches (n = 50 to n = 75)

Variations were provided in training strategies by varying treatments. The groups were:

Small Group Approaches

Group A (n=17): Only Instructional Material group.
Group B (n=18): Conventional Teaching Method group.
Group C (n=15): Training Module Approach group.

Large Group Approaches

Group D (n=57): Only Instructional Material group.
Group E (n=75): Conventional Teaching Method group.
Group F (n=51): Training Module Approach group.

Precautions were taken to minimize the threats due to internal and external validity.

Selection of Experimenters

The science teacher educators of the four colleges were asked to conduct the experiment in their respective colleges after providing them an orientation towards ITM.

Tools used in the study are

1. Willingness scale for teacher educators: A modified version of the scale standardized by Passi and Sansanwal (1985).
2. Theory check up for student teachers: This was prepared keeping in view the theoretical requirements of the ITM.
3. Reaction scale for student teachers: This scale was prepared by modifying the scale prepared by D'Lima and Sugandhi (1986).
4. Willingness scale for student teachers: This scale was an adapted version of the scale developed by D'Lima and Sugandhi (1986).

The four scales were validated by a panel of judges comprising of teacher educators from Centre for Research in Education, Nagarjuna University, Guntur. The reliability of the tools that were estimated using spilt half technique was in the accepted range.

Analysis of Data

The teacher educators' responses to the willingness scale were tested against the equal probability hypothesis using chi-square. To identify the influence of selected variables on willingness scores 't' test was done. Each item on willingness scale was analysed using chi-square test.

The student teachers responses to the three scales were analysed using ANOVA to determine if variance existed between the training strategies in terms of (i) sample size and (ii) treatment variations.

Findings and Conclusions

Teacher educators believed that models of teaching are vehicles of communication of scientific process skills. They believed in the philosophy of models of teaching as strategies to improve teacher education programmes. They acknowledged that they had knowledge of models of teaching and were aware of the need for classroom dissemination of models of teaching.

In spite of expressing the view that they were ready to implement models of teaching, they found it impracticable to implement them. The impediments they foresaw in the implementation of models were time constraints, inability of student teachers to comprehend theory of the models and lack of instructional materials.

The overall response of teacher educators was encouraging since they were willing to implement models of teaching though they had expressed some reservations.

Sex and teaching experience were not significantly influencing the willingness scores of teacher educators. Teacher educators who possessed research degrees like M.Phil., Ph.D. were more favourable in implementing models compared to those who had postgraduate degrees. Those who had attended in service programmes were more willing to implement models of teaching. Teacher educators who were handling methods of teaching school subjects were having a better disposition towards implementation of models of teaching than those handling foundation teach courses were.

The analysis of responses of student teachers showed that there is no reason to believe that small group techniques were more effective than large group techniques.

The type of training adopted made no impact on the theoretical understanding of the student teachers. The student teachers had not understood the various phases in the ITM.

The overall reaction of student teachers was positive in almost all the items. The student teachers taught by modular approach showed better reactions than those trained by conventional teaching or theoretical orientation. The student teachers were able to identify that ITM develops scientific process skills. They expressed the fear that they would not be able to formulate a discrepant event. They felt that the model requires resourceful teachers.

The student teachers were willing to implement models of teaching. They were prepared to try out ITM in their practice teaching. They were willing to encourage teachers to undergo training in ITM.

The training by modular approach was best received by student teachers in comparison to conventional teaching or theoretical orientation. It became evident that a new innovation or approach would be best received when it is presented in a systematically planned manner. Training by modular approach should be adapted to train student teachers in the use of models of teaching.

The teacher education programme should be one that satisfies the needs of the modern day schools. It is the responsibility of teacher educators to prepare science teachers who are conversant of the latest innovations. Models of teaching are examples of latest developments in the field of education whose knowledge would improve the teaching competence of student teachers. ITM could prove to be a very important tool in the hands of a resourceful teacher in teaching of science.

The present study has elicited the response of teacher educators to a willingness scale. The response pattern led to the conclusion that teacher educators are overwhelmingly in favour of models of teaching.

The teacher educators have fully realized the importance of the models of teaching and hence have shown a positive orientation to receive and implement the innovations. This is more conspicuously seen in the methods teachers, teaching physical science among other methods where a direct application of ITM was felt practicable.

While the majority of teacher educators had shown willingness to use models of teaching, those with added scholastic experience in the form of acquiring higher qualifications like M.Phil. and Ph.D. has displayed more positive disposition. Those teacher educators who had attended in service programmes had access to latest literature and exposure to innovations. Hence they had shown more willingness than those who had confined themselves to their regular professional duties only.

Inquiry skill training is one of the chief aims of science teaching. ITM is concerned with the development of Inquiry Skills. Inquiry based teaching can be introduced in schools only if there are teachers trained to implement it. The training needs to begin at the teacher education level. The first recipients are the student teachers.

In this study student teachers were trained by three different strategies. One strategy was providing them only theoretical orientation. They were supplied with a handout. The exposure to handout could also produce the same understanding of ITM on par with that produced by modular approach and conventional teaching. The novelty, variety and suspense of presentation of discrepant event in ITM evoked and sustained the same degree of interest across different presentations—theoretical, conventional and modular.

A Handout was prepared on psychological principles. It has sustained the interest of student teachers and motivated them to read through the entire contents. The contents of the handout were the descriptions of models of teaching and its utility; the different families of models; description of ITM and its phases. It also had a detailed lesson plan with a physical science example on black bodies. The handout ensured conceptual understanding of ITM.

One of the main goals of science teaching is to develop process skills. Inquiry training approach helps in developing the skills of creative thinking, scientific inquiry, divergent thinking, and independent thinking. The student teachers have a shown positive trend towards ITM and its efficacy. Their reactions show that they have acknowledged the fact that ITM develops science process skills.

On the whole, reactions shown by student teachers indicate that they have understood the advantages of the model. It is very encouraging to observe that they are having a positive reaction towards ITM which when cultivated further would yield significant dividends.

The implementation of ITM requires the willingness of student teachers to use the model. The method and its salient features impressed the student teachers and they were willing to use ITM. They were motivated to learn other models.

The modular approach has been proved to be an effective strategy to train student teachers in the use of ITM. The modular approach comprises of three parts: (i) The theoretical orientation in the form of a handout, (ii) Lecture demonstration session, and (iii) Group work and Group discussion.

The lecture-demonstration session provided a practical and intimate training. The student teachers were the subjects and they tried to account for the discrepancy in the problem presented by the teacher educators. They had a real experience of ITM in session. The teacher educators were experienced and could provide an enthralling experience to the student teachers.

The final session of group work was very useful in helping student teachers to formulate discrepant events. The student teachers could formulate examples suitable for ITM in nearly all topics of physical science.

The group discussion that completed the modular approach training strategy further augmented the understanding of different steps of ITM. The misconceptions were cleared and remedies were suggested. The two additional factors over and above the information given in the handout used greater receptiveness and even instilled required skills in implementation of ITM towards maximizing effective science teaching.

The large group samples have shown understanding, positive reactions and willingness comparable to small groups. Hence ITM can be easily introduced in teacher education programme using modular approach training strategy.

The inclusion of models of teaching in the curriculum can be recommended because there is approval from both teacher educators and student teachers. In service training for teacher educators to follow the phases of the model, to prepare lesson plans, and to prepare instructional materials is necessary. This will keep the teacher educators ready to implement as and when models are included in the curriculum.

Recommendations/Suggestions for Further Research

The present study has identified a few areas in which further research might be undertaken.

Generally, studies in models of teaching have been confined to the information processing models only. The purpose of education is not only to develop the cognitive domain. Hence, studies need to be taken up with models that can develop both affective and psychomotor domains. Feasibility and adaptability of different models for different subjects may be studied.

This study has proved the effectiveness of 'modular approach'. Further studies using this approach for other models may be attempted. The effectiveness of this 'modular approach' in skill training needs to be probed. The effectiveness of strategies in terms of student teachers competence to implement the models in actual classroom situation also can be studied.

Studies to validate techniques of preparation of self-instructional materials and lesson plan writing need to be undertaken. The use of only 'Herbartian method' can be avoided if such attempts are made.

Studies on use of educational technology in developing training strategies need to be taken up.

Some of the areas may be:

(i) Computer assisted instruction for models.
(ii) Designing programmed instructional materials.

(iii) Use of audio-visual equipment: preparation of audio lessons, video lessons, transparencies, slides, etc., for models of teaching.

(iv) Text book modification and self instructional material production.

Innovations like micro teaching, team teaching and simulation have been to some extent adopted in different teacher education colleges. Use of micro teaching for providing training in models of teaching may be studied. Use of simulation techniques in combination with models of teaching can be attempted.

A more in-depth analysis of the training needs of the three groups: teacher educators, teachers, and student teachers will enable the educationists to develop effective training programmes based on the findings of the present study.

BIBLIOGRAPHY

Adaval, S.B. *et al.* (1984). *An analytical study of teacher education in India,* Amitabh Prakashan, Allahabad, India.

Adaval, S.B. (1979). *Quality of teachers,* Amitabh Prakashan, Allahabad, India.

Aggarwal, J.C. (1995). *Teacher and Education in a Developing Society,* Vikas Publishing House (Pvt.) Ltd., New Delhi. pp. 411- 58.

Alexander, P.A. and Judy, J.E. (1988). *The interaction of domain specific and strategic knowledge in academic performance,* Review of Educational Research, Vol. 58(4), pp. 375-404.

Al-khayyat and Abdul Kareem, A. (1981). *Comparing the effects of inquiry and traditional methods of teaching social studies in two Kuwaiti secondary schools for boys,* Univ. Microfilm International Dissertation Abstracts, Vol. 41 (10) pp. 4198A - 521A.

Allen, D.W. and Ryan, K.A. (1969). *Micro teaching,* Reading Mass, Addison Wesley.

AMA, ASE, AAM. (1947) *Teaching of Science in secondary schools,* (Third edition), John Murray Publishers Ltd., London.

Anderson, *et al.* (1970). *Developing children's thinking through science,* Prentice Hall Inc, Englewood Cliffs, New Jersey.

Antimdas (1987). *Effectiveness of Training strategy in Concept Attainment Model and personality of pre service teachers training.* Trend of research and abstracts of research studies at M.Ed., M.Phil., Ph.D. and project levels at Dept of Education, Devi Ahilya Viswavidyalaya, Indore, M.P, p. 42.

Ary D, Lucy, C. Jacob., and Asghar, Razavieh. (1972). *Introduction to Research in Education,* Holt, Rinehart and Winston Inc, New York.

Banerjee, N.P. (1993). *Strategies of Educational Research,* Associated Publishers, Ambala Cantt, India.

Basu, A.N. (1952). *Indian Education in Parliamentary papers,* Part I, Asia Publishing House, Calcutta, pp. 112, 125, 177, 178, 179.

Best, W. John, and Kahn, V. James (1989). *Research in Education* 6th Ed, Prentice Hall of India Pvt. Ltd., New Delhi.

Bhagabhan, Subudhi (1991). *Inquiry training model of teaching: Effectiveness of training with variations in Demonstration and Peer Practice Feedback,* Journal of Indian Education, Vol. XVIII (4) ,pp. 42-47.

Bhaskara Rao, Digumarti, ed. (1996). *Encyclopaedia of Education for All,* 5 vols. APH Publishing Corporation, New Delhi.

Bhaskara Rao, Digumarti, ed. (1994). *International Encyclopaedia of Science and Technology Education,* 8 vols, Discovery Publishing House, New Delhi.

Bhaskara Rao, Digumarti, ed. (1996). *National Policy on Education,* 2 vols. Anmol Publications, New Delhi.

Bhaskara Rao, Digumarti, ed. (1998). *National Policy on Eduction: Towards an Enlightened and Humane Society.* Discovery Publishing House, New Delhi.

Bhaskara Rao, Digumarti, ed. (1998). *Reforming School Education.* Discovery Publishing House, New Delhi.

Bhaskara Rao, Digumarti, ed. (1998). *District Primary Education Programme.* Discovery Publishing House, New Delhi.

Bhaskara Rao, Digumarti, ed. (1998). *Teacher Education in India,* Discovery Publishing House, New Delhi.

Bhaskara Rao, Digumarti, (1998). *Teacher Education in India,* (Telegu version). Nagarjuna Publishers, Guntur.

Bhaskara Rao, Digumarti, (1996). *Teaching of Science,* (Telegu version). Nagarjuna Publishers, Guntur.

Bhaskara Rao, Digumarti, and Digumarti Pushpa Latha, eds. (1998). *International Encyclopaedia of Women,* 5 vols. Discovery Publishing House, New Delhi.

Bhatnagar, O.P. (1987). *Evaluation Methodology for Training: Theory and Practice,* Oxford and IBH Publishing Company Ltd., New Delhi, India.

Bihari S.K. (1987). *Effectiveness of training strategy in learning Concept Attainment Model at B-Ed level,* Trend Report and Abstract (1985-86), Department of Education, Devi Ahilya Viswavidyalaya Indore, M.P., p. 53.

Black and Daniel, Hugh (May 1982). *Comparison of Inquiry and Non Inquiry methods in development of critical thinking,* Univ. Microfilm International Dissertation abstracts, Vol. 42 (11), pp. 4624 – 957A.

Brown, G.A. (1975). *Teaching and Microteaching Models,* Rationale and Programme, Education for teaching, Vol. 98, pp. 71-80.

Brunkhorst., Brunkhorst, Yager, Andrew, and Apple. (1993). *The Salish Consortium for the improvement of science teaching – Preparation and development,* Journal of Science teacher education, Vol. 4, pp. 51-53.

Buch, M.B. (Ed) (1973). *A Survey of Research in Education,* M.S. University, Baroda.

Buch, M.B. (Ed) (1979). *Second Survey of Research in Education,* Society for Educational Research and Development, Baroda.

Buch, M.B. (Ed) (1987). *Third Survey of Research in Education,* NCERT, New Delhi.

Buch, M.B. (Ed) (1993). *Fourth Survey of Research in Education,* NCERT, New Delhi.

Buddhi Sagar, M. (1990). *Teaching Educational Psychology to B.Ed students – Development of instructional material by using Advance Organizer Model and Operant Conditioning Model,* Indian Educational Review, Vol. 25 (4), pp. 42-56.

Calcutta University Commission Report (1919), Vol. V, as cited in Uday Shanker (1984).

Campbell, Donald T. and Julian, C. Stanley (1963). *Experimental and Quasi Experimental designs for Research on teaching, in Handbook of Research on teaching,* Gage, N.L. (Ed), Rand McNally and Company, Chicago, pp. 175, 176.

Carin, A. Arthur and Robert, B. Sund (1970). *Teaching science through discovery.* Charles E. Merill Publishing Company, Ohio.

Carl, A. Grant (1982). *Bringing teaching to life – An Introduction to Education,* Allyn and Bacon Inc, Boston.

Carl, Maria J. (1981). *An evaluation of the effectiveness of Inquiry instruction to foster creativity in intermediate grade students,* Univ. Microfilm International dissertation abstracts, Vol. 42, pp. 428-8938.

Chadda, D.K. (1991). *Dimensions of teacher education,* Anmol Publications, New Delhi.

Chauhan, S.S. (1979). *Innovations in teaching learning process,* Vikas Publishing House (Pvt.) Ltd., New Delhi.

Chaurasia, G. (1979). *Challenges and Innovations in Education,* Sterling Publishers (Pvt.) Ltd., New Delhi.

Chermat, K. and Jerome, Steven (1981). *The relationship between the Inquiry teaching Process and student achievement in advanced placement American History classes,* Univ. Microfilm International Dissertation Abstracts, Vol. 41, No: 621, pp. 2332A - 904.

Chitriv, U.G. (1988) *Evaluating Differential Effectiveness of Ausubel and Bruner and Strategies for Acquisition of concepts in Mathematics.* In Ausubel Vs Bruner.

Models for teaching Mathematics, Himalaya Publishing Company.

Chube, S.P. (1985). *Features of comparative education,* Vinod Pustak Mandir, Agra.

Clive, Lindop (1971). *Evaluating Effectiveness in Teacher Education,* Journal of Education for teaching, Vol. 11 (2), pp. 165-76.

Conant, James Bryant (1963). *The Education of American Teachers,* McGraw Hill Book Company Inc, p. 218.

D'Lima, and Sugandhi, R. Prabhu. (1986). In *Inquiry Training Model* of teaching by Passi, B.K., *et al.*, pp. 47-65.

D'Lima, C.G. and Lobo Clifton. (1985). *In Inquiry Training Model of Teaching* by Passi, B.K., *et al.*, pp. 46, 51, 52.

D'Lima, Lobo and Sugandhi. (1986). *Inquiry Training Model : A Skill Based Approach,* Disney Enterprises, Bombay.

Das, B.C. (1993). *Effectiveness of Concept Attainment Model in terms of teaching competency of pre service student teachers,* Perspectives of education, Vol. 9(1).

David Jacobsen *et al.* (1981). *Methods for Teaching – A Skills Approach,* (Second Edition), Charles. E. Merrill Publishing Company, Ohio.

David, McNamara (1990). *Research on teachers thinking: Its contributing to educating student teachers to think critically,* Journal of education for teaching, Vol. 16(2), pp. 147-60.

Deborah, J. Trumbull and Patrica, Kerr. (1993). *University researchers' inchoate critiques of Science teaching: Implications for the content of Pre service science teacher education.* Science Education, Vol. 77(3), pp. 301-17.

Devegowda, A.C. (1973). *Teacher Education in India,* Printersall (P) Ltd., Bangalore.

Discussion document – Curriculum framework for teachers education (1996). NCERT, Delhi, p. 16.

Dow, Gwyneth (1979). *Learning to teach – Teaching to learn,* Routledge and Kegan Paul, London.

Dress *et al.* (1960). *How the Individual Learns Science,* as cited in William. K. Esler (Jr.), (1980).

Dubey, Alpana (1986). *A study of the efficacy of the Inquiry Training Model in learning outcomes,* Unpublished M.Ed Dissertation, Univ. of Indore.

Duncan, Anita and Samuel, Ralph. (1949). *New Directions in Science teaching.* McGraw Hill Book Company Inc., New York.

Ebel, R.L. (Ed) (1969). *Encyclopedia of Educational Research,* The Macmillan Company, London.

Ediger, Marlow and Digumarti Bhaskara Rao (1996). *Science Curriculum*. Discovery Publishing House, New Delhi.

Edmund, Amidon and Elizabeth, Hunter (1966). *Improving Teaching*. Holt, Rinehart and Winston Inc., New York.

Eggen, D. Paul, *et al.* (1979). *Strategies for teachers – Information Processing models in the classroom*, Prentice Hall Inc., New Jersey.

Eggleston, J.F., Galton, M.J. and Jones, M.E. (1976). *Process and Products of Science Teaching*, Macmillan Education, London.

Elliot, J. Labbett, B. (1975). *Teaching research and teacher education*. Some comments on CBTE, Education for teaching, Vol. 96, pp. 51-61.

Eunice, Boyd and Kenneth, D. George. (1973). *Effect of Science Inquiry on the abstract categorization behaviour of deaf children*, Journal of research in science teaching, Vol. 10(1), pp. 91-99.

Frank, Smith and Harrison, H.S. (1965). *Principles of class teaching*, English Language Book Society and Macmillan and Co. Ltd., London.

Gage, N.L. (Ed) (1964). *Handbook of research on teaching*, American Educational Research Association, Third Printing, RandMcland and Company, Chicago, pp. 43-46.

Garrett, E. Henry and Woodworth, R.S. (1985) *Statistics in Psychology and Education* Eleventh Indian Reprint, Vakils, Feffer and Simons Ltd. Bombay.

Gary, L. Sweitzer and Ronald, D. Anderson. (1983). *Meta Analysis of Research on science teacher education practices associated with inquiry strategy*, Journal of Research in Science teaching, Vol. 20(5), pp. 453-66.

George, Brown (1978). *Lecturing and Explaining*, Methuen and Co Ltd., London.

Gerald, W. Lott (1983). *Effect of Inquiry teaching and Advance Organizer upon Science Education*, Journal of Research in Science teaching, Vol. 20(5), pp. 437-51.

Getleri, Andrew and John, Smyth (1989). *Teacher evaluation: Education alternatives*. Palmer Press, East Sussex.

Ghosh (1986) as quoted in *Fourth Survey of Research in Education*. Buch, M.B.Ed., (1993).

Good, Carter. V. (1966). *Essentials of Educational Research Methodology and Design*, Appleton Century Crafts, New York.

Good, Carter .V. (1973). *Dictionary of Education*, McGraw Hill Book Company, New Delhi.

Goyal, J.C. (1985). *The Indian Teacher Education, Some Characteristics*, National Psychological Corporation, Agra, India.

Grewal, S.S. (1988). *Teacher Effectiveness*, Prakash Brothers, Ludhiana, India.

Guilford, J.P. (1965). *Fundamental Statistics in Psychology and Education*, McGraw Hill Book Company, New York.

Gulati, K.C. (1987). *A study of the factors associated with teachers predisposition to adopt educational innovations*, in Third Survey of Research in Education, NCERT, New Delhi, p. 806.

Gupta, S.K. (1983). *Technology of Science Education*. Vikas Publishing House (Pvt.) Ltd., New Delhi.

Gupta, K. Arun. (1984). *Teacher education – current and prospects*, Sterling Publishers (Pvt.) Ltd., New Delhi.

Hans, Brugelman (1975). *Lost in the desert of Innovation Theory – The Mirage of dissemination and implementation*, Education for teaching, Vol. 98, pp. 49-61.

Hilligard, F.H. (1971). *Teaching the teacher trends in teacher education*, George Allen and Unwin Ltd., London.

Hogben, D. and Lawson, M.J. (1984). *Trainee and beginning teacher: Attitude, stability and change*, Journal of education for teaching, Vol. 10(2), pp. 135-53.

Hopkins, David and Reid, Reno (1985). *Rethinking Teacher Education*, Croom Helm (Ltd.), Kent.

Howard and Audrey, Nicholas. (1975). *Creative teaching*, George Allen and Unwin, London.

Ian, Lewis (1975). *Teaching training – Professional or Peripheral*, Education for teaching, Vol. 96, pp. 35-42.

Jaus, H. (1975). *The effects of integrated science process skill instruction on changing teacher achievement and planning practices*, Journal of Research in Science teaching, Vol. 12, pp. 439-47.

Jean, Ruddock (1985). *Teacher research and Research based teacher education*, Journal of Education for teaching, Vol. II (3), pp. 291-99.

John, Bratholemer (1985). *Theory and Practice: An as yet un-addressed Issue*, Journal of Education for teaching, Vol. II (3), p. 281 - 89.

John, Brown (Ed) (1986). *Science in Schools*, Open University Press, Milton Keyes, Philadelphia.

John, Oslon. (1992). *Understanding teaching expertise*, Open University Press, Buckingham.

John, H. Clarke and Arthur, W. Biddle (1993). *Teaching Critical Thinking – Reports from Across the curriculum*, Prentice Hall Inc, Englewood Cliffs, New Jersey.

Johnston, D.T. (1963). *School teaching*, Robert Hale Ltd., London.

Johnston., Susanne., Craig. (1980). *Identification of some relationships between Piagetian operations at levels of science achievement by Junior High School students in science classes categorized as Inquiry and Non-inquiry oriented*, Univ. Microfilm International Dissertation Abstracts, Vol. 41 (5), pp. 1812A-2327A.

Joyce, Bruce and Weil, Marshal (1992). *Models of teaching* (4th Edition) Prentice Hall of India (Pvt.) Ltd., New Delhi.

Jyoti, R. Ugru (1990). *Effects of Inquiry training on Process skills and achievement in Biology*. Unpublished M.Ed. dissertation, Regional Institute of Education, Mysore.

Kalyani, Raghavan and Robert, Glaser. (1995). *Model based Analysis and Reasoning in Science – MARS curriculum*, Science Education, Vol. 79 (1), pp. 37-61.

Kamlesh, Chaudary (1986-87). *An exploratory study to identify skills of CAM and ITM and to test the study feasibility of using a skill based approach to training of Pre service teachers in these models*, Thoughts and Experiments in secondary teacher education, NCERT, New Delhi.

Kamlesh, Chaudary (1989). *Teaching of Concepts through CAM and facts through traditional teaching – Competency of teaching skills of pre service teachers*, Indian Educational Review, Vol. 24(4), pp. 105 - 13.

Katiyal, Sunita (1985). *How does Inquiry Training Model affect the learning outcomes in comparison to traditional teaching*, Unpublished M.Ed dissertation, University of Indore, Indore.

Kaul, Lokesh (1993). *Methodology of Educational Research*, Vikas Publishing House (Pvt.) Ltd., (Reprint, Second Edition).

Kerlinger, N. Fred (1973) *Foundations of Behavioural Research*, 2nd Ed, Holt, Rinehart and Winston Inc, New York.

Kishor, M. Shah (1983). *Innovative teacher*, Shilpa Prakashan, Vidyanagar, Gujarat, India.

Kochar, S.K. (1990). *Methods and techniques for teacher*, (2nd edition). Sterling Publishers (Pvt.) Ltd., New Delhi.

Koehler, V. (1985). *Research on Pre service teacher education*, Journal of teacher education, Vol. 36, pp. 23-30.

Korthagen, F.A.G. (1985). *Reflective teaching and Pre service teacher education in the Netherlands*, Journal of teacher education, Vol. 36(5), pp. 11-15.

Kremer, L. and Perlberg, A. (1979). *Training of teachers in strategies that develop independent learning skills in pupils*, British Journal of teacher education, Vol. 5 (1), pp. 36-47.

Kuethe, L.K. James (1984). *The teaching learning process*, Scott, Foresman and Company, Glenview, USA.

Kuslan, Louis., and Stone, Harris. (1968). *Teaching children Science – An Inquiry approach*, Wadsworth Publishing Company Inc, Belmont, California.

Lakshmi, S. (1989). *Challenges in Indian Education*, Sterling Publishers (Pvt.) Ltd., New Delhi.

Lakshmi, Ravikanth . A. (1984). *Information Processing Models of Teaching – Cognitive Models: An Analysis*, The Education Review, Vol. XCV (2).

Lazarowitz, R., Barufaldi P.J., and Huntsberger, P.J. (1978). *Student teachers characteristics and favourable attitudes towards Inquiry*. Journal of Research in science teaching, Vol. 15 (6), pp. 559 - 66.

Lazarowitz, R. and Lee, Addison (1976). *Measuring Inquiry attitudes of Secondary Science teachers*. Journal of Research in Science teaching, Vol. 13, pp. 455-60.

Learning to be (1972). UNESCO Document as cited in Aggarwal J.C. (1995) p. 414.

Leonilla, Menehes (1989). *Effect of Inquiry training on Inquiry skills, creativity and Achievement in History*, Unpublished M.Ed. dissertation, Regional Institute of Education, NCERT, Mysore.

Lewis, D.G. (1968). *Experimental Designs in Education*, University of London (Pvt.) Ltd., London.

Mani, R.S. (1985). *Inquiry Training Model of teaching: An overview*. Indian Educational Review, Vol. 20(4), pp. 51-65.

Maya, Talvi and Digumarti Bhaskara Rao, eds. (1996). *Educational Leadership and Social Changes*. Discovery Publishing House, New Delhi.

Mathur, V.S. (1975). *Teacher Education – Some Thoughts*. Aggarwal Parkashan, Ambala City.

Mayer, R. (1989). *Models for understanding*. Review of educational Research, Vol. 59 (1), pp. 43-64.

McCleland., Alan V. and Verma, Ved (1989). *Advances in teacher education*, Routledge and Kegan Paul, London.

McAdams., William Dossett (1980). *Comparison of structured and Inquiry instructional approaches in affecting eighth grade students understanding of and response to the persuasive language usage in the media*, Univ. Microfilm International Dissertation Abstracts, Vol. 41, No 1, pp. 2A-436A.

Michael, Bassey (1975). *A paradigm for Analysing teaching*. Education for teaching, Vol. 98, pp. 61-70.

Michael, Naish and Anthony, Hartnett. (1975). *What theory cannot do for teachers,* Education for teaching, Vol. 96, pp. 12-19.

Mishra, A.K. (1983). *On Science and Science Education,* School Science, Vol. XXI (4).

Mohanty, Jagannath (1992). *Current Issues in Education,* Cosmo Publications, New Delhi.

National Policy of Education - 1986 (with modifications undertaken in 1992), Ministry of Human Resource Development, Dept of Education, Publication No. 1723, pp. 44- 45, New Delhi. (1992).

Nemar, Medhat (1980). *Ahmed Meta Analysis of the outcomes of Biology as Inquiry,* Univ. Microfilm International Dissertation Abstracts, Vol. 40, No: 11, pp. 5630A-6043A.

Panchal, B.R. (1979). *A study of innovative proneness of teacher educators of secondary teachers training colleges of Gujarat State,* No: 629, Second Survey of research in Education (1972-78) p. 440.

Pandey, A. (1987). *Teaching style and concept attainment in Science.* Third Survey of Research in Education (1978-83), p. 769.

Passi, B.K., Singh, L.C. and Sansanwal, D.N. (1987). *Inquiry Training Model of teaching,* National Psychological Corporation, Agra.

Passi, B.K., Singh, L.C. and Sansanwal, D.N. (1993). *Implementing Training strategies and studying effectiveness of different Variations in Components of Training strategy for ITM in terms of understanding, Competence, Reaction and willingness of student teachers,* 4th Survey of Research in Education in India, pp. 970, 971.

Patil, V.C. and Patil, B.C. (1982). *Problems in Indian Education,* Oxford and IBH Publishing Company, New Delhi.

Paul, E. Adams and John, W. Tillotson (1995). *Why Research in the Service of Science teacher education is needed?* Journal of Research in science teaching, Vol. 32(5), pp. 441-43.

Perlberg, A., Kremer, L. and Lewis, R. (1979). *Towards new teacher education models,* British Journal of teacher education, Vol. 3, pp. 263-81.

Peter, Dawson (1984). *Teachers and teaching.* Basil Blackwell Ltd., Oxford.

Peters, Burnett and Farnell (1963). *Introduction to teaching,* Macmilan Company, New York.

Peterson, A.D.C. (Ed) (1965). *Techniques of teaching,* Voi. 1, Pergamon Press, Oxford.

Peterson, D. Kenneth (1978). *Scientific Inquiry Training for High School students: Experimental Evaluation of a model programme,* Journal of Research in Science teaching, Vol. 15 (2) pp. 153-59.

Postlethwaite, Keith (1989). *Teaching and teacher education*. Progress through Inquiry, Oxford Review of Education. Vol. 15(1), pp. 93-98.

Progress of Education in India, 1912-1917, Vol. II, p. 178 in Uday Shanker. (1984).

Purkait, B.R. (1987). *New Education in India*. The Associated Publishers, Ambala Cantt, India, 370-75.

Ramaswamy. R. (1993). *An Inquiry into correlates achievement*. Karpoorampathippagan Publications, Madurai, India.

Rao, Digumarti Bhaskara and K. R. S. Sambasiva Rao, eds. (1996). *Current Trends in Indian Education*. Discovery Publishing House, New Delhi.

Rath, K.B. (1983). *Validation of teaching models: Need for empirical data*, Journal of Indian Education, Vol. IX (1), pp. 3-7.

Rathaiah, Lavu and Digumarti Bhaskar Rao, eds. (1997). *International Innovations in Education*. Discovery Publishing House, New Delhi.

Report of the Chattopadhyaya Commission on Secondary School Teachers (1983-85) as cited in Aggarwal J.C (1985) pp. 422-24.

Report of the Indian Education Commission, 1882, p: 254 in Uday Shanker. (1984).

Report of the Education Commission, 1964-66 (1970) NCERT, New Delhi.

Report of the Secondary Education Commission, 1952-53, Govt. of India Publications. Report of the Education Commission, 1964-66, NCERT, New Delhi.

Review of Education in Bombay State (1855-1955), Bombay Government Printing, p. 283 (1958) in Uday Shanker. (1984).

Richard, L. Campbell (1979). *A comparative study of the effectiveness of process skill instruction on reading Comprehension of Pre service and In service elementary teachers*. Journal of research in science teaching, Vol. 16 (2), pp. 123-29.

Richie, J.A. (Ed) (1984). Selection from Educational records Vol. II, p. 38, Calcutta in Uday Shanker.

Robert, B. Stevenson (1991). *Action Research as professional development: An U.S. Case study of Inquiry oriented in service education*. Journal of education for teaching, Vol. 17 (3), pp. 277-92.

Robert, Millar (Ed) (1989). *Doing Science, Images of Science in Science Education*, The Falmer Press, New York.

Rodriguez, Imelda. and Lowell, J. Bethel. (1983). *An Inquiry approach to Science and language teaching*, Journal of Research in Science teaching, Vol. 20(4), pp. 291-

Romey, D.William (1968). *Inquiry techniques for teaching science* Prentice Hall International.

Ronald, J. Bonnsletter (1992). *Science teacher education – The necessity of variety in teaching*, Science education International, Vol. 3 (3), pp. 29-31.

Rowe, Mary Budd (1978). *Teaching Science as a Continuous Inquiry* – A Basic, McGraw Hill Inc. USA.

Roy, Nash (1973). *Classrooms observed, the teachers perception and pupils performance*, Routledge and Kegan Paul, London.

Saadeh, I.Q. (1969). *The teacher and development of critical thinking*, Journal of Research in Development and education, Vol. 3, pp. 87-99.

Saddler, J.E. and Gillet, A.N. (1970). *Training for teaching – A three-year course*, George Allen and Unwin Ltd. (Fourth Impression), London.

Sarah, Guri., and Rozenblit (1990). *Four models of teacher training in Israel: Some lessons and Implications for teacher educators*, Journal of Education for teaching, Vol. 16 (3), pp. 225-33.

Sarason, Seymour. B., *et al.* (1962). *The preparation of teachers*, John Wiley and Sons Inc, New York.

Schnur, J.O. and Golby, M.J. (1995). *"Teacher Education – A University mission"*. Journal of teacher education, Vol. 46, pp. 11-18.

Science Masters Association—London (1947). *Teaching of General Science*, John Murray (Publishers) Ltd.

Sharma, H.L. (1989). *School Science Education in India*. Commonwealth Publishers, New Delhi.

Sharma, R.A. (1989). *Teacher Education – Theory, Practice and Research*, International Publishing House (Pvt.) Ltd., Meerut, pp. 61-67.

Shukla, R.S. (1978). *Emerging trends in teacher education*, Chugh Publications, Allahabad, India.

Siddiqi and Siddiqi (1988). *Teaching of Science – Today and Tomorrow*, Doaba House, New Delhi.

Sidhu, K.S. (1987). *Methodology of Research in Education*, Sterling Publishers (Pvt.) Ltd., (Second Reprint) New Delhi.

Simon, H.A. (1975). *Models of thought*. Yale University Press New York.

Singh, R.P. (1993). *The challenges of tomorrow: A profile of future teacher's education*, Sterling Publishers (Pvt.) Ltd. New Delhi. (1993).

Singh, Ajit (1990). *Training of student teachers in the models of teaching: Relative effectiveness of different training strategies,* Indian Educational Review, Vol. 25 (4), pp. 27-41.

Singh, Amrik. (1993). *The trap called teaching – Reflection's on teaching and teachers,* Konark Publishers (Pvt.) Ltd., New Delhi.

Singh, Amrik. (Ed) (1995). *The craft called teaching.* Konark Publishers (Pvt.) Ltd., New Delhi.

Singh, Bhoodev (1986). *Teaching competence and attitude towards teaching of prospective teachers: Effect of teaching models,* Indian Educational Review, Vol. 21 (4), pp. 16-24.

Sivakumar, P. and Prema, P. (1997). *Effectiveness of Suchmans Inquiry Training model in learning Biology.* Journal of Educational Research and Extension, Vol. 33(3), pp. 136-40.

Smith, B.O. (1995). *Towards a theory of teaching teachers,* College Press, Columbia in Aggarwal, J.C. (1995) p. 414.

Smith, Elmer R. (1962). *Teacher Education,* Harper and Row Publishers, New York.

Srinivasan, V. (1985). *Innovative Educational Programmes – Some Hurdles.* Journal of Indian Education, Vol. X (6), pp. 30-33.

Srivastava, Anand P. (1987). *Teaching and learning in XXI Century,* Learning Laboratories Publication, New Delhi.

Srivastava, R.C. and Bose, K. (1963). *Theory and Practice of teacher education in India.* Chugh Publications, Allahabad, India, pp. 32-41.

Srivastava, R.C. (1997). *Teacher Education in India: Issues and Perspectives,* Regency Publications, New Delhi.

Stahl, Abraham (1991). *Bridging the gap between research and teacher education – An Israeli Innovation.* Journal of Education for Research. Vol. 17 (3), pp. 293-300.

Stinnet, T.M. (1965). *The profession of teaching,* Prentice Hall of India (Pvt.) Ltd., New Delhi.

Suchman, J.R. (1960). *Rebuilding the Science programme: Inquiry training in the elementary school,* Science teacher, Vol. 27.

Sund, R.B. and Trowbridge, L.N. (1967). *Teaching Inquiry in Secondary Schools,* Charles E. Merill Book Inc, USA.

Surjeet, Singh (1985). *Inquiry approach in the teaching of science in school,* School Science, Vol. XXIII (3), pp. 10-16.

Susandhya, Mohanty (1996). *Teaching of Science in Secondary Schools,* Deep and Deep Publications, New Delhi.

Sushma (1987) *Effectiveness of concept Attainment Model and Biological Science Inquiry Model for teaching Biological Science to VIII Class students.* Department of Education, BHU.

Teacher Education Curriculum – A Frame Work, (1996). Draft resolution, National Council for Teacher Education (1978) in Curriculum Frame work for teacher education – Discussion Document, NCTE, New Delhi.

Third Survey of Secondary teachers education in India (1971-72), NCERT Publications, New Delhi. (1979).

Tibble, J.W. (1971). *Future of teacher education,* Routledge and Kegan Paul, London.

Toffler, Alvin (1985). *Future Schools* in Aggarwal, J.C. P: 415.

Travers, Robert M.W. (1978). *An Introduction to educational research,* Macmillan Publishing Company Inc, New York.

Travers, Robert. M.W. (1973). *The Handbook of Research on teaching,* Rand McNally & Co, Chicago.

Uday, Shanker (1984). *Education of Indian teachers,* Sterling Publishers (Pvt.) Ltd.

UNESCO - ILO Document. *Status of teachers* 1967 in Aggarwal J.C. (1985) : p. 414.

University Education Commission Report - 1949, Govt. of India, p. 210 in Uday Shanker (1984).

Valand, J.B. (1983). *A study of Innovative Proneness of teachers of Primary teachers training colleges in the state of Gujarat,* 4th Survey of Research in education, NCERT, p. 1003.

Vasistha, K.K. (1979). *Teacher education in India.* Concept Publishing Company, New Delhi.

Vernon, S., Gerlach, and Donald, Ely P. (1980). *Teaching and media: A systematic approach,* Prentice Hall Inc, Englewood Cliffs, New Jersey.

Voss, B.E. and Brown, S.B (1968) *Biology as Inquiry: a book of teaching* methods as cited in William, C. Kyle (JR) (1976) pp. 2.

Walker, W. (1967). *World Trends in Education* in Aggarwal. J.C. (1985) p. 414.

Whitney, Frederick L. (1964). *The elements of Research,* Prentice Hall Inc, Englewood Cliffs, New Jersey.

William, K. Esler (1973). *Putting it all together – Inquiry process, science concepts and the text book,* Science education, Vol. 57 (1), pp. 19-23.

William, C. Kyle (Jr.). (1980). *The distinction between Inquiry and scientific Inquiry and why High School students should be cognizant of the distinction,* Journal of Research in science teaching, Vol. 17(2), pp. 131-37.

Wilson, J.T. and Koran, J.J. (1976). *Effects of generating hunches on subsequent search activities when learning by inquiry,* Journal of Research in Science teaching, Vol. 13, pp. 1-10.

Wilson, J. (1974). *Processes of scientific Inquiry: A model for teaching and learning science,* Science education, Vol. 58; pp. 127-33.

Wubbles, Th. and Korthagen, F. A.G. (1990). *The effects of pre service teacher education Programme for the preparation of reflective teachers.* Journal of Education for teaching, Vol. 16 (1), pp. 29-43.

Zeichner, K.M. and Liston, D.P. (1987). *Teaching student teachers to reflect,* Harvard Educational Review, Vol. 57, pp. 23-48.

APPENDIX - A

HANDOUT ON INQUIRY TRAINING MODEL OF TEACHING FOR B.ED. STUDENTS

1. What is a model of teaching?

A model of teaching is a 'blue print' from which teaching techniques are developed. Models of teaching are meant for creating a good classroom climate. They not only effect learning in a given subject, but also teach students how to think in that subject. Bruce Joyce and others have developed ways of putting the learning theories into practice. Each model has a rationale that justifies it and describe what is suitable and why.

2. Why are teaching models necessary?

The aims of the teaching-learning process are to help the students to grow emotionally, physically, socially, and intellectually. To achieve these multiple objectives the teachers are required to be engaged in several professional roles. To prepare the teachers for a variety of roles, Bruce Joyce and Marsha Weil have researched on a variety of techniques and learning theories and designed a number of models of teaching.

3. What are the different types of teaching models?

The models of teaching are organized into four families based on their emphasis, i e., the educational goals and means. They are-

a. *Information processing models*: They provide an orientation towards the information processing capability (thought process) of students and ways they can improve their ability to master and retain information. Models included here are: Inductive thinking, Inquiry training, Scientific inquiry, Concept attainment, and Cognitive growth, Advance organizer and Memory model.

b. *Social Interaction Models*: They emphasize on the relationship of individual to the society and other persons. The models included here are: Social inquiry, Group investigation, Social inquiry, laboratory method, Jurisprudential, Role playing and Social simulation.

c. *Personal models*: They provide an orientation towards the individual and development of selfhood. The models included here are: Non-directive teaching. Awareness, Synectics, Conceptual systems and classroom meeting model.

4. *Behaviour Modification models*: They have evolved from attempts to develop efficient systems for sequencing learning tasks and shaping behaviour by manipulating reinforcement. Models included here are—Relaxation, Programmed instruction, Managing behaviour, Anxiety reduction, Assertive training, Simulation and Directive training.

4. What are the stages in the description of model?

There are four stages in the description of a model. They are:

i *Syntax*: It describes the model as a flow of actions. It is described in terms of sequence of events, which are called phases.

ii *Principles of reaction*: They guide the teacher's response to the learner.

iii *Social system:* It refers to the additional requirements beyond the usual human skills, capacities and technical facilities necessary to implement a model.

iv *Support system*: It refers to the additional requirements beyond the usual human skill capacities and technical facilities necessary to implement a model.

5. What is a discrepant event?

A discrepant event is a problem, which is contrary to their conceptual system. It should encourage data gathering and hypothesis testing. It involves illogicality that conflicts the notion of reality. Every puzzling situation cannot be a discrepant event. It may be puzzling because there is no new concept or we do not know the answer. The problem should be one that has a 'cause effect' relationship.

6. What is Inquiry Training Model (ITM) of teaching?

The "Inquiry Training Model" (ITM) was designed by Richard Suchman (1962) to teach students how to learn an inquiry process. A discrepant event is presented to the students. They gather data by asking Yes/No answer type questions. Using the data gathered they develop hypothesis and formulate theory to account for the discrepancy. Finally, they analyze the inquiry process followed and suggest analogies.

7. What is the Syntax of ITM?

There are five phases in the Syntax of ITM:

1. Encounter with the problem.
2. Data gathering—Verification.
3. Data gathering—Experimentation.
4. Formulation of an explanation.
5. Analysis of Inquiry process.

8. What are the principles of reaction of ITM?

In ITM, the most important reactions of the teacher take place during the second and third phases. The teacher should assist the students to inquire, but should not do the inquiry for them. He should see to it that questions are properly phrased and not vague. He should not disapprove any theory proposed. He should encourage interactions among students.

9. What is the social system of ITM?

The social system here is co-operation. The model is based on assumption that team approach is better than individual approach. ITM requires an open classroom climate where the teacher acts as an instructional manager and monitor. The students are active throughout the model.

10. What is the support system of ITM?

The main requirements of ITM are a set of discrepant events, teacher's knowledge about the inquiry process, and resource material related to the problem.

11. What are the Instruction and Nurturant effects of ITM?

Instruction effects of ITM are:

1 Developing scientific process skills.
2. Strategies for creative inquiry.

Nurturant effects of ITM are:

1. Developing spirit of creativity.
2. Autonomy in learning.
3. Tolerance of ambiguity.
4. Understanding the tentative nature of knowledge.

12. What are the four levels at which theory building can take place in ITM?

Suchman suggested the following levels of theory building:

1. Simple linear causation
2. Theories of properties.
3. Analogies.
4. Application of generalization or principle.

APPENDIX - B

LESSON PLAN FORMAT FOR ITM

Topic: Radiation of Heat in Black Bodies

PHASE 1: Explanation of Inquiry Procedure and Encounter with the Problem

(a) Generating opening moves to initiate the first phase of the model.

We are going to play a new game today. Everyone should participate in this game. I will present a puzzling situation and you will solve the puzzle following the rules of the game.

(b) Explanation of the Inquiry procedure:

Here are the rules of game:

(i) I will present a discrepant problem to you.
(ii) You will ask questions to gather more information about the problem.
(iii) The questions that you ask must be framed in such a way that my answer should be Yes/No.
(iv) When you have gathered enough data you should make guesses regarding the solutions.
(v) You can then ask questions to test these guesses.
(vi) You will ultimately have to find out the solution to the problem.

(c) Encounter with the problem presentation of the discrepant event.

Two teams A and B were playing a football match in Madras. Team B was taking part in the tournament for the first time whereas team A had won many trophies in the past. In no way was team B a match for team A. Team A made a very good start but to everybody's surprise team A lost the match". Why?

PHASE 2: Data Gathering/Verification

(a) Verify nature of objects and conditions:

QUESTION	RESPONSE
Were some main players in team A injured?	(No)
Did team B players use any drugs?	(No)
Did team B have the advantages of home crowd cheering them?	(No)
Did team A players suffer from jet lag?	(No)
Did team A and team B wear dresses of same material?	(Yes)
Were the dresses of same colour?	(No)
Did team A wear dark clothes?	(Yes)

(b) Verify nature of occurrence of problem situation

QUESTION	RESPONSE
Was the match held in Summer?	(Yes)
Were players of team A of different country?	(Yes)
Did team A play another match on the same day?	(Yes)
Did team A players sweat a lot?	(Yes)
Did team B players sweat a lot?	(No)

PHASE 3: Data Gathering / Experimentation

(To isolate relevant/ irrelevant variables)

QUESTION	RESPONSE
If team A and B had interchanged their dresses would team A have won?	(Yes)
If the game was played in Jammu would team A have won?	(Yes)
Do players of team A sweat so profusely in their home country?	(No)
If team B plays team A in winter in the same venue will it win?	(Yes)
Were teams A wearing black shirts?	(Yes)

PHASE 4: Hypothesis Formulation and Explanation

(a) Simple team causation:

"Team A lost the game because they were wearing black shirts".

(b) Theories of properties:

Black bodies absorb heat. Because players of team A wore black shirts that did not reflect the absorbed heat of the summer noon, they were sweating profusely. This caused them discomfort and as a result they felt exhausted and lost the game.

(c) Analogies:

1. People prefer to wear white coloured cotton clothes in summer.
2. The solar cookers are painted black.

PHASE 5: Recapitulation and Discussion

(a) Recapitulation of steps of inquiry:

(i) Understanding the Inquiry procedure and problem.
(ii) Asking fact-finding questions.
(iii) Asking experimentation questions to test their hypothesis.
(iv) Formulating an explanation.

(b) Discussion of Elements of Inquiry:

Why did you ask question relating to:

(i) Nationality of players.
(ii) Colour of the dress.
(iii) The venue / season.
(iv) The sweating of team A players.

APPENDIX - C

WILLINGNESS SCALE FOR TEACHER EDUCATORS

Sir/Madam,

Improving educational standards involves changes in the process of classroom teaching. The need of the hour is to develop new instructional strategies. "Models of teaching" are one such important innovation in this direction. A model of teaching is like a blue print from which teaching strategies are developed. This questionnaire is to know your opinion on this innovation. The data will be kept confidential and used for research purpose only. Your co-operation is solicited.

Thanking you,

Your sincerely,

Researcher

Please give the following information.

1. Name of the institution where you are working:
2. Age:
3. Sex:
4. Educational Qualifications:
5. Teaching Experience:

   (a) As a teacher educator
   (b) Any other type of teaching experience

6. Subjects taught at B.Ed. level:
7. No. of theory classes handled per week.

8. Practical work handled at B.Ed. level
9. (a) Did you attend any in service programme:
   (b) Number of programmes attended
   (c) Nature of programmes

10. Have you registered for: M.Phil. or Ph.D.

Please encircle the response given against the statement:

(A- Agree, N-Neutral, D-Disagree)

No.	Statement	Response		
1.	I have knowledge of the models of teaching.	A	N	D
2.	I find the models of teaching are more effective than the existing methods of teaching.	A	N	D
3.	I do not understand the theory underlying the models.	A	N	D
4.	I have lost faith in educational innovations.	A	N	D
5.	Models of teaching are difficult to implement.	A	N	D
6.	Implementing Models of teaching is time consuming.	A	N	D
7.	Adequate facilities for implementing models of teaching are not available in my institution.	A	N	D
8.	The instructional materials for implementing 'Models of teaching' are not available.	A	N	D
9.	I can implement models of teaching in spite of several limitations.	A	N	D
10.	I am ready to implement models of teaching provided my workload is reduced.	A	N	D
11.	The inclusion of models of teaching can improve teacher-training programme.	A	N	D
12.	Student teachers will find it difficult to understand the theory of the models of teaching.	A	N	D
13.	The use of models of teaching in teacher education curriculum is not practicable.	A	N	D
14.	Implementation of models of teaching will not have any financial implications.	A	N	D
15.	Models of Teaching are not new as the salient features are already found in the existing methods.	A	N	D
16.	Research on models of teaching should be disseminated for classroom implementation.	A	N	D

APPENDIX - D

ITM THEORY CHECK UP FOR STUDENT TEACHERS

Dear friend,

Improving educational standard involves changes in the process of classroom teaching. The need of the hour is to develop new instructional strategies, design ways to implement them and to develop training strategies to train the student teacher. This questionnaire is to gather your opinion about one such training strategy. The data will be kept confidential and used for research purpose only. Your co-operation is solicited in this academic venture.

Thanking you,

Yours sincerely,

Researcher

Please fill in the following personal data:

1. Name of Teacher trainee:
2. Date of Birth: Date: Month: Year:
3. Your educational Qualification:

No	*Degree*	*Name of. Institution*	*Subjects offered*	*Class obtained*	*Medium of Instruction*
(a)	Graduation				
(b)	Post Graduation				

4. (a) Where did you do your Schooling? Rural / Urban
   (b) Where did you have your collegiate education? Rural / Urban
5. Teaching Methods: Subject offered: (a)
   (b)

I. Choose and tick (✓) the best response.

1. Inquiry means....
   (a) to read out textual matter
   (b) to describe an event
   (c) to investigate and solve a problem
   (d) to listen to teachers instruction
2. A discrepant event is....
   (a) An unexpected event
   (b) An undisputed event
   (c) A routine event
   (d) A chance event
3. Inquiry training model (ITM) was designed by....
   (a) Richard Suchman
   (b) Ausubel
   (c) Hilda Taba
   (d) Skinner
4. An inquiry training class requires....
   (a) Active participation by all students
   (b) Explanation to be given by teachers
   (c) Laboratory work to be performed by students.
   (d) Passive listening by students.
5. In ITM students gather data by....
   (a) manipulation of facts
   (b) direct experimentation
   (c) questioning (yes/no answer type questions)
   (d) taking teachers guidance and using books.
6. Which of the following describes Suchmans rule?
   (a) Students cannot hypothesize a possible explanation till the end of Inquiry class.
   (b) Students cannot refer to books during the inquiry session.
   (c) The teacher clarifies and explains when students ask for it.
   (d) Students gather data by asking questions, which are answerable by Yes or No.
7. The correct response of a teacher in an inquiry class is....
   (a) Wait, Don't give explanation till I ask you to
   (b) Your hypothesis is marginally correct. Try again.

(c) Don't discuss among yourself. Work independently.
(d) Now let us analyze your questions. Why did you ask "..." question?

8. The ITM is reoriented towards....
   (a) The development of emotional behaviour of pupil.
   (b) The development of relationship between individual and society.
   (c) The development of scientific process skills and creativity.
   (d) Shaping of behaviour by manipulating reinforcement.
9. An inquiry session ends only after....
   (a) A hypothesis is proposed.
   (b) Teacher suggests a possible explanation
   (c) Analysis of inquiry session is made
   (d) Data is gathered by asking Yes/No answer type question.
10. The following is an example suitable for an inquiry lesson....
    (a) A science teacher wants students to know the difference between solute and solvent.
    (b) A science teacher wants students to know why people prefer to wear cotton clothes in summer.
    (c) A science teacher wants to teach the students the usefulness of group learning.
    (d) A science teacher wants students to know the time span of formulation of a star.
11. The following is an inappropriate question in an inquiry session.
    (a) Are the objects identical in shape?
    (b) Is one of the objects denser than the other?
    (c) If I paint both the objects, will the same effect be observed?
    (d) What material is used to make the objects?
12. The following is an instructional effect of I T M?
    (a) Development of scientific process skills.
    (b) Development of social adjustment.
    (c) Development of creativity.
    (d) Development of independence or autonomy of learning.

II Match the following:

(a) Match the stages of description of teaching model with stage number

Stage Number	*Name of Stage*	*Response*
(a) One	1. Support system	( )
(b) Two	2. Social system	( )
(c) Three	3. Principle of reaction	( )
(d) Four	4. Syntax	( )

(b) Match the phases of syntax of ITM with phase number:

Phase Number	*Phase*	*Response*
(a) One	1. Analysis of Inquiry process	( )
(b) Two	2. Encounter with the problem	( )
(c) Three	3. Data gathering—verification	( )
(d) Four	4. Data gathering—Experimentation	( )
(e) Five	5. Formulation of an explanation	( )

APPENDIX - E

REACTION OF STUDENT TEACHERS TOWARDS ITM

Please circle your response given after each statement: (A - Agree, N – Neutral, D – Disagree.)

No.	*Statement*	*Response*		
1.	I find it difficult to formulate a discrepant event	A	N	D
2.	I think it is difficult to understand the process of pupils through this model	A	N	D
3.	A teacher will be more active while teaching through ITM compared to ordinary teaching	A	N	D
4.	Creative thinking of children can be stimulated through this model of	A	N	D
5.	It is suited to the present class room setting 60 to 70 students	A	N	D
6.	It makes pupils alert and attentive	A	N	D
7.	I do not feel competent to handle various phases of the model	A	N	D
8.	The model teaches pupils not to respond without thinking	A	N	D
9.	This model teaches pupils to view a situation from various angles	A	N	D
10.	This model develops the spirit of scientific inquiry among students	A	N	D
11.	There is a chance of pupil getting frustrated when they are not able to find the solution	A	N	D
12.	It discourages the pupils from thinking that theirs is the only right answer	A	N	D
13.	Strict adherence to the rules of the model destroys the pupils creative spirit	A	N	D
14.	It is time consuming, yet there is no thorough understanding of the subject matter	A	N	D
15.	This model gives a sense of participation to each child	A	N	D
16.	This model is not suited to the present day school curriculum	A	N	D

{Cont.}.....

17.	It discourages rote learning	A	N	D
18.	The model teaches pupils to delay conclusions	A	N	D
19.	The model teaches pupils to ask pinpointed questions	A	N	D
20.	Discipline in the classroom cannot be maintained while using this model	A	N	D
21.	This model provides freedom to student for independent thinking	A	N	D
22.	Implementation of this model requires a change in examination system	A	N	D
23.	This model requires resourceful teachers	A	N	D

APPENDIX - F

WILLINGNESS OF STUDENT TEACHERS TO IMPLEMENT THE MODEL (ITM)

Please encircle the response given against the statement:

(Y – Yes, N - No, U - Undecided)

No.	*Statement*	*Response*		
1.	Are you ready to use the model in your practice teaching even if it is not insisted upon by your college supervisor?	Y	N	U
2.	Will you continue this model even if your first inquiry fails?	Y	N	U
3.	Will you use this model when you become a regular teacher?	Y	N	U
4.	Would you like to learn other models of teaching?	Y	N	U
5.	Would you encourage regular teachers to undergo training in ITM?	Y	N	U